THE SMALL
OFFSHORE YACHT

OTHER BOOKS OF INTEREST

The Offshore Yacht
A. T. Thornton
ISBN 0 229 11681 7

Seaworthiness: The Forgotten Factor
C. A. Marchaj
ISBN 0 229 11673 6

The Symmetry of Sailing
Ross Garrett
ISBN 0 229 11759 7

Designer's Notebook: Ideas for Yachtsmen
Ian Nicholson
ISBN 0 229 11801 1

Icarus: The Boat that Flies
James Grogono
ISBN 0 229 11803 8

IN PREPARATION

Design Your Own Yacht
Ben Smith
ISBN 0 229 11760 0

Sailing Theory and Practice 3rd edition
C. A. Marchaj
ISBN 0 229 11819 4

THE SMALL
OFFSHORE YACHT

Tim Thornton

ADLARD COLES LIMITED
8 Grafton Street, London W1

Adlard Coles Ltd
William Collins Sons & Co. Ltd.
8 Grafton Street, London W1X 3LA

First published in Great Britain by
Adlard Coles Ltd 1987

British Library Cataloguing in Publication Data

Thornton, Tim
    The small offshore yacht.
    1. Yachts and yachting
    I. Title
    797.1'24   GV13

ISBN 0-229-11794-5

Typeset by V & M Graphics Ltd, Aylesbury, Bucks
Printed and bound in Great Britain by
R.J. Acford Ltd, Chichester

CONTENTS

FOREWORD

I often wondered what someone interested in sailing offshore in a small yacht would need to read to guide him in the right direction. I now know he should read *The Small Offshore Yacht*.

It is obviously impossible to learn everything overnight, but it is an advantage to be told the basic principles of naval architecture which apply to a small yacht, and have them explained in such a simple fashion, as in this book. I am sure this book will increase your understanding of some boats' behaviour and help you to choose the right boat, as well as teaching you what to do in the middle of the ocean. I am also convinced that your better understanding of 'what makes a boat tick' will allow you to enjoy it more and that is very important.

As I was reading the book, I was particularly impressed by Tim Thornton's coverage of what is, in fact, a vast subject. I think there is some superb advice for anyone just about to buy a small offshore yacht, and it will be good reading even for those who think they know it all – helping them to improve their sailing and their boat.

I am going to keep a copy on my shelf and I advise you to do the same.

Tony Castro

THE DEVELOPMENT OF THE SMALL YACHT

A *thumbnail history of yachting*

Yachting began in the seventeenth century, when gentlemen started using workboats and naval vessels to go out sailing for pleasure. In time these boats developed into designs aimed specifically at pleasure sailing, though the hull forms still showed their workboat roots. The naval connection may still be seen in the Royal Yacht Squadron, Britain's most exclusive yacht club, whose members have the right to fly the Royal Navy's White Ensign. The boats tended to be heavy displacement, due to the simple construction methods of the day, and long-keeled with low sail area and low freeboard. Although very seakindly, in as much as their hull form enabled them to lie a-hull for long periods in heavy weather, they lacked the responsiveness that appeals to many modern sailors, low sail area made them sluggish in light airs, and the low freeboard meant that the decks were often swept by waves when at sea. The actual word 'yacht' originated from the Dutch *jaght* and German *jacht*, meaning 'hunting' or 'chasing', and first applied to a breed of fast sailing workboats.

All the yachts in use at this stage were considerably larger than the small boats (under 32 ft/9.8 m LOA) which we will be looking at. However, they did start the evolution towards the modern yacht form. Freeboard became higher for a drier boat and, although they still had a full-length keel, the ends of the boats became finer and the midship section evolved from a box section to the classic wineglass, giving much better performance to windward.

Right from the start, there was a difference in hull form between the two sides of the Atlantic. The European yachts and workboats were generally full-ended with almost semicircular midship sections, designed more for carrying capacity than anything else. The American boats, on the other hand, were largely designed for speed, being fine-ended with a V-ed midship section and hard bilges, and often with a centreboard to cope with the many shallow harbours and sounds.

At the same time during the nineteenth century, open dayboats developed to form the basis of dinghy sailing and the various metre yacht classes (in fact, the One Ton Cup was first competed for by boats of this type, before it was adopted by the offshore racers). However, there was very little, if any, sailing of small boats equipped for more than day sailing.

In fact, it was not until almost the middle of the nineteenth century that small yachts began to make an impact, partly because it was not until then that the open seas were free enough of pirates and brigands for small craft to be able to travel in safety. The first person to cruise extensively in a small yacht was Richard McMullen, who first of all cruised the south coast of England in the 20 ft (6.1 m) LOA sloop *Leo* between 1850 and 1857. Then he moved up to the 32 ft (9.8 m) cutter *Sirius* in which he sailed round Britain in 1863, amongst other voyages. In the end he died at sea of a heart attack when crossing the Channel in his 27 ft (8.2 m) yawl *Perseus*. Shortly afterwards in 1869, Edward Middleton circumnavigated Britain in a 23 ft (7 m) yawl. Ocean crossings also occurred, a 26 ft (7.9 m) iron square-rigged lifeboat was sailed across the Atlantic from west to east by two Americans as a publicity stunt for their design; and a 20 ft (6.1 m) converted lifeboat, *City of Ragusa*, crossed from east to west with a two-man crew in 1870 (a slow passage of 84 days). From this point onwards, cruising boomed, and by the end of the century many boats had circumnavigated Britain, and sailed the downwind route from America to Europe. However, it took considerably longer for the racing fraternity to realise that small yachts could be seaworthy, and to accept them in their offshore events.

It was also around this time that owners realised that larger boats inevitably sailed faster than smaller ones, and so various handicapping formulae were created. These developed from the merchantman's tonnage rules, which estimated the number of tuns (or barrels) that would fit in the hold, generally as a function of length, beam, and sometimes the depth of the hold. The only one of these rules to stand the test of time is Thames Measurement, once used by the Royal Thames Yacht Club for their handicapping system, and sometimes still used to indicate the size of a cruising yacht. The formula (in feet) is:

$$\frac{(L-B) \times B \times \frac{1}{2}B.}{94}$$

No sooner had rating rules been introduced than owners and designers tried to take advantage of them. The first step here was to rake the stern backwards, as length was measured along the keel. This gave a shorter length, but poor steering characteristics (even though a raked stern is often seen as one of the features of the ideal traditional cruising hull form). At the same time, over slightly more than ten years, length:beam ratios rose from 3.5 to an incredible 6.2, in an attempt to lower the rating through less beam. In order to try and retain sufficient stability, length:draft ratios went from 5.6 to 4.2, and displacement:length ratios rose from 270 to 330 ton/cu.ft (9.7 to 11.8 t/cu. m), with the extra weight going into a heavy deep keel. Thus, right from the start racing yachtsmen have not really been interested in fast or seaworthy boats, but simply in boats which are fast in relation to their handicap.

At the same time a different approach was being followed in North America, as American rules were based on multiplying the waterline length by the sail area. This approach then spread to Europe, as a reaction against the shortcomings of the rules based on length and beam. With no limit on beam or displacement, the obvious line of development here was to keep the weight of the boat to a minimum, and to obtain the necessary stability through a shallow, beamy hull. The search for less weight meant that freeboard was reduced to a minimum, and long overhangs were included so that the boat rapidly increased her sailing length as she heeled. Moreover, advances in the new science of naval architecture meant that the detrimental effect of excessive wetted surface area had been discovered, and so the separate fin keel was developed, often with a bulb on the bottom. As this moved the rudder further forwards, handling problems became increasingly severe, until designers realised that the rudder had to be separated from the keel and moved it right aft. By the end of

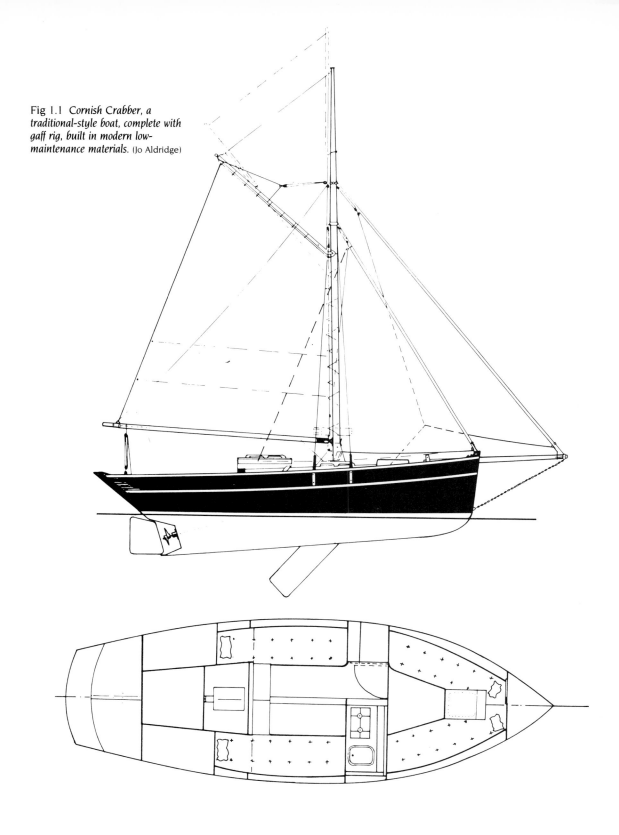

Fig 1.1 *Cornish Crabber, a traditional-style boat, complete with gaff rig, built in modern low-maintenance materials.* (Jo Aldridge)

the century these boats were really very similar to today's International Offshore Rule (IOR) boats, except for the longer overhangs and lower freeboard. However, due to the heavier hull construction the centre of gravity was considerably higher, and it was not unknown for these boats to capsize on their moorings.

Whilst these extreme racing yachts were developing, cruising designs were quietly evolving along lines nearly independent of the racing fleets – though not totally so, as American cruisers, too, tended to be lighter and beamier than their British equivalents. Cruising boats had a waterline length:beam ratio of 3:1 or 4:1, displacement:length ratios of 175 to 225 ton/cu. ft (6.3 to 8.1 t/cu. m), and sail area:displacement ratios of around 50 to 75 sq. ft/ton (4.6 to 6.9 sq. m/t). Moderately long overhangs were maintained to help the bows rise to waves, and a long keel was kept, with an almost straight profile from the forefoot to the rudder stock, combined with the classical wineglass section. A further lesson, learnt from the so called 'plank-on-edge' length–beam formula boats, was that just as much stability was gained through a low centre of gravity as through a wide, boxy midship section. Thus, cruising yachts started carrying more and more of their weight in a ballast keel, and beam was reduced slightly as a result. (Initially there were some doubts as to the effect of such a heavy, static weight in the boat, and this resulted in some owners mounting the ballast on springs.)

Meanwhile, the racing fraternity decided to turn its back on the excesses of the earlier, simpler rules, and a new style of rule evolved which was based on length, beam, sail area and the hull girth, measured amidships. This last factor penalised boats with wide, shallow hull sections and those with fin keels, as opposed to those whose keel faired into the hull form. This penalty on boats with hollow garboards was later taken even further by also incorporating the girth difference, between a skin girth measured along the hull and a chain girth taken by stretching a string round the hull and pulling it tight, so that it bridged any hollows in the hull.

The style of racing was also changing. Up until now, both dayboats and boats fitted out with full accommodation had just raced round an inshore course. In 1906 Thomas Fleming

Day changed all this by organising the first Newport to Bermuda race for cruising yachts, and this race is still one of the American classics. In Europe the Royal Ocean Racing Club (RORC) was formed in 1925 by the committee that organised Europe's first major offshore race, the Fastnet Race, and on both sides of the Atlantic the sport of offshore racing quickly flourished.

By 1920 the International Rule had been developed, for use in both Europe and the United States:

$$\text{Rating} \quad \frac{(L + B + \frac{1}{2}G + 3d + \sqrt{SA} - F)}{2.5}$$

where L is length, B beam, G measured girth, d girth difference, SA sail area and F freeboard. In the 1930s G and B were dropped from the formula and the divisor was changed from 2.5 to 2.37, and this has remained the basis of the rule for the 6- and 12-metre classes (fig. 1.2), with a few extra restrictions on draft and displacement. Note that beam is no longer penalised, except indirectly by the increase in both G and d that would result from an increase in beam, and for the first time a rating benefit is given for high freeboard. This line of thought marked the first time that the rule-makers decided to formulate a rule that would generate boats of moderate hull form, and not just create a new framework for exploitation.

Whilst this rule governed the development of day-sailing keelboats, on the offshore scene the British adopted the American Universal Rule in 1912 and developed it to become the RORC rule . Basically the same as the later IOR rule, it penalised length, sail area and stability, whilst giving a benefit to heavy displacement, measured by multiplying beam by hull depth. Stability was not measured directly, but rather assessed by a scantlings section in the rule, a boat with heavy scantlings being given a rating benefit due to her assumed loss in stability. Meanwhile, in the USA the Cruising Club of America (CCA) rule embodied a new approach, having a set of ideal proportions and adding or subtracting factors for beam, draft, displacement, sail area, freeboard, stability and engine installation, where these differed from the ideal. The boats produced were relatively heavy and undercanvassed, with a displacement:length ratio of 300–400 ton/cu. ft (10.8–14.4 t/cu.

Fig 1.2 *6-metre yacht. The combination of girth difference measurement and relatively heavy displacement result in this deep, narrow hull form.*

m). A similar approach was also followed in the International Cruiser/Racer rule, which produced the cruising counterpart to the day racers of the International Rule. On the one hand, the RORC rule tried to handicap any yacht fairly, whatever her proportions; on the other hand, the CCA and International Cruiser/Racer rules were heavily type-forming, penalising any boat that strayed too far from the rule maker's ideal boat. Thus, the latter were much more restrictive for the designer, but probably also resulted in a more stable rule.

Whilst hulls and rating formulae were developing, changes were also taking place on the sail plan side. Although the first Bermudan rig appeared in 1875, it took until the 1920 Olympics for it to prove its superiority to windward over the gaff rig, and the gaffers were often faster downwind. Moreover, although the large, full balloon jib had been used when sailing downwind for a number of years, the first use of the modern-day genoa for windward as well as offwind work occurred in 1927. Although it was less efficient in terms of mere sail area, the handicap rules measured only the foretriangle area, so any overlapping headsail gained a considerable amount of unrated area.

By this time, marine engines had become reliable enough – and small enough – for the motor sailer to be developed. Until now, the size of marine engines meant that motor vessels had to be relatively large, and although sails were often fitted they were generally only steadying sails, used to damp the rolling motion under power. It still took many years for the sailing fraternity to accept having an engine in a boat as a matter of course, though.

During the 1950s there were about half a dozen single-handed circumnavigations, with a widely varying number of stops *en route*, in boats of 20 to 30 ft (6.1 to 9.1 m) LOA. By the 1960s the austerities of the post-war years were over. The development of plastic construction made yachting affordable by more people than ever before, and the gradual change to a more leisure-based society has meant that cruising has boomed. Crossing the Atlantic is not seen to be anything like as adventurous an exploit as it once was.

On the racing side, it still took the Royal Ocean Racing Club until 1947 to admit boats with a waterline length of less than 24 ft (7.3 m) to their races, regarding them as unseaworthy. As a result, the Junior Offshore Group (JOG) was started as a breakaway organization to provide racing for these small boats. Now history is coming full circle as JOG races tend to be more popular than RORC events (except for international events), and there are those within the RORC who want to try and bring

JOG under its wing. It is also interesting to note that right from the start JOG had a rule requiring a certain minimum righting moment from a knockdown, based on the boat's dimensions and ballast ratio, a problem that the IOR has only really tried to get to grips with in the past few years.

Perhaps the most well-known of the early JOG boats was *Sopranino*, 19 ft 8 in (6 m)long, with 5 ft 4 in (1.6 m) beam, with 160 sq. ft (14.9 sq. m) of sail and a displacement of 1,550 lbs (700 kg). Definitely a lightweight boat even by today's standards, with a displacement:length ratio of 129 ton/cu. ft (4.6 t/cu.m), and also well canvassed at a ratio of 232 sq. ft/ton (21.2 sq. m/t), her extensive racing and transatlantic voyages finally proved that size and weight are not necessarily essential to make a boat seaworthy. Even so, it still took until 1973 for the RORC to introduce Class VIII for boats rating below Quarter Ton (about 26 ft (7.9 m) LOA).

On the true ocean racing scene, Blondie Hasler's junk-rigged 25 ft (7.6 m) Folkboat *Jester* has been the only boat to enter every single OSTAR (*Observer* Singlehanded TransAtlantic Race) from the first one in 1960, and many small boats, some as small as 19 ft (5.8 m) LOA have competed.

In 1966 the French invented the concept of level-rating classes with the revival of the One Ton Cup, for boats rating up to 22.0 ft under the RORC rule. Many yachtsmen appreciated the opportunity to race on level terms with the rest of the fleet without the complications of time allowances, and the idea quickly spread to produce the five level-rating classes we currently have. It is here, with the regular world championships in each class, that the forcing point of offshore yacht design and sailing is to be found. (The IOR rule is now used instead of the RORC rule.)

By 1961 the racing fraternity had had enough of having different rating formulae on different sides of the Atlantic, and in 1970 the IOR rule was introduced – a mixture of the RORC and CCA rules. The final impetus to welding the two rules together was the possibility of having offshore racing in the Olympic Games. The basic formula is

$$\text{Rating} = \left[0.13 \left(\frac{L \times S}{\sqrt{B \times D}} \right) + 0.25L + 0.2S + DC + FC \right] \times EPF \times CGF$$

Fig 1.3 Folkboat, quite possibly the most successful cruising boat of all time, still in production despite the limited accommodation. (Jo Aldridge)

where S is the square root of the sail area, B×D estimates the
boat's weight through the cross-sectional area of the hull
amidships, DC and FC are small corrections for freeboard and
draft, EPF gives compensation for an engine, and CGF taxes
stability. The original aim was to be able to rate fairly all
designs, and the rule-makers tried to keep ahead of the rule-
cheaters by quickly getting on to Mark III and Mark IIIA of the
rule, much modified to plug the loopholes. However, eventually they limited their aims to keeping the rule stable and
preserving the existing fleet.

In the last few years the expense of owning and campaigning
an IOR yacht at high levels of competition has risen very
rapidly, as has the standard of those sailing these craft.
This has resulted in a number of recent developments
aimed at giving offshore racing a wider appeal. The first of
these was the development of one-design classes such as the
Sonata, J-24 and Sigma 33. Their one-design nature keeps
costs down and keeps the resale value of the boats at a
reasonable level. It also enables the designs to be of a
different style to the IOR, either more orientated towards
cruising, like the Sonata or Contessa 32, or lighter and more
dinghy-style, like the J-24.

Another development is that a large number of local
handicap rules have arisen, most notably the American PHRF
(Performance Handicap Rating Factor) system, Skandicap in
Scandinavia, and the RORC–UNCL (Union National pour la
Course au Large) Channel Handicap in Britain, France and the
Far East. For the most part these are uncomplicated rules,
aimed almost entirely at production boats and sailing at club
level. The ORC (Ocean Rating Council), creators of the IOR, are

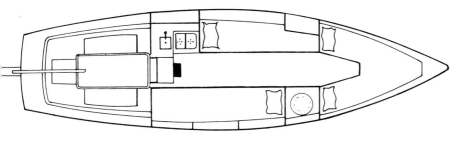

also pushing their answer, the IMS (International Measurement System), developed under the name MHS (Measurement Handicap System) in the USA; but the high cost of the complex measurement required means that the rule is unlikely to catch on for small keelboats, though it is popular in the USA, where the average size of boat is comparatively large. Finally, perhaps the most significant move by the ORC is that it has permitted sponsorship and advertising in IOR races, removing the need for wealthy individual owners, and also further distancing the upper echelons of the sport from the average club sailor.

In conclusion, we can say that the history of offshore racing yacht design is in essence the history of handicapping formulae – as soon as boats started being handicapped, the designers shaped the hulls and rigs to exploit the rule under which the boats sailed. In most cases this was pushed to the point where the boats became unsailable, unseaworthy or both, whereupon a new rule was developed and the whole cycle began again. Cruising boats have tended to copy the trends of racing designs in a more moderate form, and the classic cruising yacht of an age tends to be the racing yacht of the previous one.

Construction developments

Until comparatively recently, sailing was a sport for the privileged few, and the reason for this lay more in the building costs than in the limited appeal of the sport. For most of the sport's life, having a boat built meant having a one-off boat – generally carvel or clinker-built in wood, with each piece having to be shaped individually by craftsmen. Even if several boats were being built to the same design, the cost benefits to the owners were very small. Furthermore, once built, the vessels required a high level of maintenance, partly due to the construction method used and partly due to the lack of high-performance protective finishes now available.

Initially, the boat was planked either with all the planks butted against each other, in carvel form, or overlapping, as in clinker planking. The seams between the planks were either caulked with pitch and oakum, or, if the quality of construction

Fig 1.4 X-boat being built using traditional methods, as required by the class rules. (Photo Jo Aldridge)

was good enough, the planks simply butted against each other, relying on the wood swelling up as it absorbed water to seal any small gaps. In all cases, the longitudinal planking needed to be supported by a large number of closely spaced transverse frames. These spread the load from each individual plank, prevented the hull from distorting when subjected to longitudinal loads, and also supplied all the transverse strength to the structure.

Originally, grown frames were often used, which came from trees that had been specially trained to grow into an approximation to the required shape. These frames were very strong, as the grain ran nearly parallel to the frame throughout its length, though clearly the supply was limited and they were difficult to produce. Thus, when good-quality steel became available, mild steel angle was used instead of grown frames.

Not all the frames needed to be this strong, though, and two or three lighter frames were often placed between each major frame. These smaller frames were generally made by bending a straight length of wood into shape, helped by heating the timber in a steam box to soften it, and applying it to the hull while still hot. Once in place, the frame was fastened to the planking with copper nails and roves. Oak was the traditional timber to use due to its ease of bending and resistance to rot, and this resulted in huge oak plantations in areas such as the New Forest.

Timber construction slowly developed through the years, and some very light boats could be built, such as the clinker-built *Sopranino*. Spar construction, too, evolved from the single solid piece of wood to the hollow wooden spar, made of four pieces glued together. The highpoint was probably achieved after the First World War, when McGruers made cold-moulded spars by wrapping a veneer round a mould several times until the required thickness was achieved, a method originally developed for the struts between the wings of biplanes.

With the advent of high performance adhesives after the Second World War, there was a minor revolution in boatbuilding. Frames could be made up by laminating veneers together, and hulls could be produced with much higher structural strengths through strip planking or cold moulding. As well as improving the structural properties of the boat, it meant that lower grades of timber could be used, since areas of poor quality could be cut out, due to the smaller sizes of timber required. Moreover, the development of plywood meant that flat surfaces such as decks or interior joinery could be built up in a fraction of the time that was formerly possible. The use of plywood was not restricted to the deck and interior, though: many small hard-chine boats were designed to use plywood for the hull, thus making home construction possible for people, with a much lower level of skill than was previously required.

In the 1960s, however, a revolution swept through the boatbuilding industry. The advent of GRP construction meant that, once a set of moulds had been built, hulls and decks could be produced quickly and cheaply by relatively unskilled labour. Furthermore, as well as reducing the cost of buying a boat, the new material required much less maintenance than timber. The form of construction also brought about boats that

Fig 1.5 *This Vega 27 under construction shows the extensive use of internal mouldings to provide the bulk of the interior.*
(Photo Tony Castro)

were totally watertight for the first time. At the same time, aluminium (light alloy) spars and synthetic sails meant that the rig was cheaper, more reliable and more suited to mass production.

Nowadays plastic is used almost universally for building the hull, and plastic internal mouldings are often used as well to form the basis of the interior or the headlining. Then the interior is finished off with plywood joinery, that is prefabricated off the boat and then dropped in for bonding in place. Once the bulk of the interior has been fitted, the deck is dropped on and secured, and the boat is virtually complete. This production line approach means that boats can be built much more cheaply than before, but it also means that the manufacturer must sell a larger number of boats to a given design in order to cover his tooling costs. It also means that there is less room for customising a boat to suit the owner's precise requirements. This is particularly the case at the bottom end of the market, where the boat is built almost entirely from GRP mouldings, with some flat ply sheets screwed to the mouldings for worktops, locker fronts and so on. Generally, the more internal joinery in a boat, the more expensive it will be, and some yards take this to the logical conclusion of offering just a bare hull and deck moulding with no more fittings than you specifically request.

As the main cost of fitting out a hull is the labour cost, most builders offer hulls in various stages of completion, from a bare hull and deck with just the structural items fitted, to an almost complete boat where all the owner has to do is bolt on the fittings. Kits of parts, or at least construction drawings, are generally available to help you complete the boat. Thus it is possible to select a boat with the hull, deck and rig that best meet your needs and fit it out yourself, saving money and, if you want, incorporating your own interior design.

One-off yachts are still built, though, for a number of reasons. On the racing front, the demand for the latest design, together with the smaller market, means that one-off designs dominate the front of the fleet, though many owners overestimate the benefits of a one-off against a carefully prepared semi-customised production boat.

Cruising-oriented one-offs may be built to give the owner his dream boat, or to save money, or simply to give the owner the pleasure of sailing a boat that he has planned and built completely from scratch. Even if professionally built, careful design and supervision of the project can keep the cost of getting it on the water down to no more than ten per cent more than the cost of a production boat. The boat may be built in GRP, usually with a balsa or foam core, or it may be built in wood. In this size of boat, hard-chine plywood construction is ideally suited to the home builder, though it seems to have gone out of fashion in favour of cold-moulded or strip-planked construction. By using epoxy resin as an adhesive and as a protective coating encapsulating the timber, wooden boats can be made both watertight and relatively maintenance-free, though because of their past record they tend to have a lower resale value than a GRP boat.

On the production boat side, we are now on the verge of yet another major revolution, not in construction materials, but in production techniques and the basic approach to design. Originally, even production boats in GRP were designed and built in the same way as traditional wooden craft, with experience forming the basis of design and construction. Now an increasing number of boatyards are pouring much greater resources into the initial design and development of new models, researching the market to ensure that the sales will be there, and modifying the concept as necessary. Then the design is tank-tested as a matter of course, and the laminate for both the main hull and deck, and all the interior mouldings, is analysed in great detail, both to ensure adequate strength and rigidity, and to minimise wastage of labour and materials. Furthermore, the boat's designers, whether an independent firm of naval architects or boatyard staff, will produce detailed drawings and a full specification for the entire vessel before

Fig 1.6 Computer-aided design systems such as this are being used by an increasing number of designers, as they allow much more detailed design work to be done before the boat enters production.
(Photo Ron Holland Yacht Design)

production begins. They thus ensure that the entire production process is carried out in the most efficient manner, and that the design complies with the increasing amounts of legislation being produced by many countries.

This approach obviously requires much more money to be invested before production begins, and so it is really only used by the larger yards at present, who have the necessary capital and sales network to sell enough boats to recoup the increased design and development costs. The designers will also tend to be a larger firm use computers for structural calculations, resistance and powering, stability, IOR and IMS rating, and probably drafting as well (see fig 1.6). The benefits of this approach are a much better design, due to the greater amount of thought which has gone into it, and lower production costs. Against this, though, in time yacht design will probably follow the course of car design, where all manufacturers tend to follow the same design trends and the number of truly individual designs is relatively small, differences tending to be due mainly to different standards of fitting out and equipment.

The spectrum of small yacht design

As small yachts represent a meeting point of dinghies and dayboats, larger yachts and workboats, there is probably a greater variety of design possibilities than in any other size range. This is increased by the low cost of building small boats, which means that a small yard does not have to be able to produce a design in such large numbers to make it worthwhile.

First of all, there are the boats modelled on successful traditional designs: for example, the Folkboat (fig 1.3) is still a successful cruising and racing class over 40 years after the first one was built. Then, there are the cruising yachts like the Vertue (fig 6.1), designed by Laurent Giles in the days when full-length keels were mandatory. Finally, there are designs based on local workboats, such as the Cornish (see fig 1.1) and Drascombe ranges. These often sport a traditional rig as well as hull form, and their large deck space combined with low interior volume mean that they are generally best suited to weekend sailing in sheltered waters.

Fig 1.7 *Westerly Konsort. The large doghouse, high-volume hull and moderate sail plan make this a typical motor sailer.*
(Photo Westerly Yachts Ltd)

Moving on from the traditional sailing workboats, we come to the motor sailers (fig 1.7 and 1.8), whose hull forms are generally derived from moderately heavy-displacement fishing boats and workboats. The deep hull sections, high freeboard and large coachroof of these boats mean that there is plenty of accommodation down below, with full standing headroom in even the smallest boat. When combined with the interior steering position this provides very comfortable sailing, even in a somewhat unpredictable climate. The heavy displacement also gives a slow, easy motion in waves. The tendency to roll in cross seas, inherent in the hull form, is reduced by the sails, often helped by bilge keels. Although the sail plan is generally too small for good light airs performance, it will still push the boat along comfortably in anything of a breeze. The underlying assumption is that with the large engine and efficient three-bladed propeller you will generally be under power in light winds. Performance also probably suffers somewhat when beating from the absence of an efficient keel.

The mainstream of designs in this size range are moderately light-displacement cruiser–racers, sold in great profusion by all the major boatbuilders. The rig is large enough to give good performance in all conditions, but not so large that the boat becomes unmanageable for the average sailing family. There are likely to be a number of keel options, ranging from a standard deep-draft keel, through a fixed shallow-draft keel or bilge keels, to a centreboard or lifting keel.

On the smaller boats the chances are that the fixed keel will be retractable, so that the boat can be put on a trailer, permitting the owner either to tow it to new cruising grounds or to dry sail it, avoiding the cost of a mooring or marina berth. On some boats, such as the Etap (fig 5.1), trailing is made much easier by a double bottom. When the boat is ashore this is empty, reducing the towing weight; once the boat is launched, a valve is opened and the double bottom fills with seawater, increasing the boat's weight to give her the necessary stability; when the boat is pulled out again, opening the valve enables the water to drain out as the boat comes up the slip.

This feature has the further benefit of giving the boat a much better chance of survival if she gets holed, as both the hull and

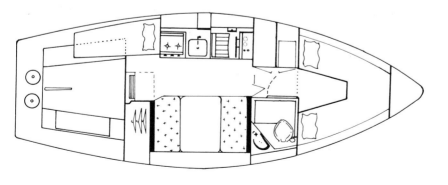

Fig 1.8 Cox 27, *a motor sailer in the style of a small yacht, complete with deckhouse and interior steering position.* (Jo Aldridge)

the double bottom need to be sprung before the boat will lose her buoyancy. On the safety side, an increasing number of builders and designers are realising that small boats are more prone to capsizing in rough seas than larger ones, due simply to the relative size of the waves compared to the boat's length and weight. Accordingly, they fit sufficient foam buoyancy between the hull and the interior moulding, or inside the boat itself, to guarantee that the boat will remain afloat if swamped or holed. It is worth checking that this has actually been tested, though, as the buoyancy needs to be carefully positioned to ensure that the boat remains afloat on an approximately even keel and with reasonable reserves of stability. If your boat has this buoyancy fitted, there may be no need to carry a liferaft on board, except perhaps for offshore journeys.

The accommodation on most production boats consists of double berths in the bows and stern, with settee berths in the saloon, and a galley, chart table and heads compartment. There is only a limited amount of interior volume in a hull, however, and each designer will have utilised it in a different way. Thus, some will have crammed in a large number of berths, ideal for flotilla sailing holidays perhaps, but too cramped unless the crew spend most of their time on deck or ashore when not sailing. Others may give a very spacious interior which may work well for a small crew, so long as it has been achieved by reducing the cockpit size or number of berths, rather than by omitting most of the stowage space. Here, one will have to assess one's particular sailing needs, and assess how successfully each design meets them.

Finally, we come to the more performance-oriented designs. First of all, there are the so-called ULDBs (ultra-light-displacement boats), which are essentially dinghies with lids on. Their lightness makes them great fun to sail, though there is a tendency for them to be tender upwind in a breeze unless beamy enough for the crew to keep them upright. Moreover, in light airs their moderate sail plan, combined with the high wetted surface area of their wide, flat hull sections, makes their performance a bit sticky. Also, on the racing side, most rating formulae penalise the light displacement relatively severely, probably because they underestimate the ill effect of the reduction in stability and the poor light airs performance.

Perhaps the best racing is to be had in the various one-design classes. Racing boat-for-boat ensures good tactical sailing and avoids the anomalies of a handicapping system. The design does not even need to be fast, so long as the standard of racing and the fleet size are high enough. Furthermore, the presence of a strong fleet means that the boats tend to hold their resale value well, while the initial outlay is much more moderate than in open classes such as the IOR, where building to a one-off design and equipping the boat with all the latest high-technology equipment is becoming more and more expensive each year. Often the class rules restrict the sail materials or the extent of instrumentation that can be fitted to the boat, with the sole intention of keeping the costs of racing under control.

Finally, there is the IOR rule which has dominated yacht racing for many years now. Although at world championship level it still provides the highest standard of competition, the gulf between the levels of sailing ability and sizes of budget of those at the top and bottom of the fleet is widening every year. More and more club sailors are becoming disillusioned with the rule, changing over to other systems such as Channel Handicap. Now that the IOR is opening up to sponsorship, though, it will probably quickly develop into a much smaller fleet, where the bulk of the boats carry sponsorship, and attract the very best sailors. However, if it is to survive this transition the measurement procedures and race administration need to be tightened up much more: there is still the remains of the attitude that sailing is a gentleman's sport, and all gentlemen will play the game by the rules. Unfortunately, as anyone who has competed in a world championship event will know, this is no longer the case.

2

HULL AND RIG DESIGN

When a designer starts planning a new creation, initially he thinks in terms of basic factors such as length, sail area, displacement, beam and stability. There is no ideal combination of these factors that will meet all weather conditions and all the needs of the yachtsman, and so the designer's craft is to find the best compromise for his client.

The three factors that must be weighed up for all boats are the ratios of sail area to resistance and sail area to stability, and the overall seaworthiness of the design. In addition, in a racing boat or cruiser-racer the handicapping rule to which the boat is designed will have a very major effect on the design, but we shall leave out this consideration for the moment.

What is meant by speed?

Just about every owner likes to think that his boat has a good turn of speed, but exactly what this means is seldom defined. To begin with, if one wants absolute speed one had better give up sailing and buy a powerboat, or better still an aeroplane. If we then assume that we want a sailing boat that is fast in relation to another, similar craft, then we have to decide whether we want a high maximum speed or a high speed in given wind conditions. Furthermore, is this performance wanted on all points of sailing or just in one direction? From the looseness of this concept of speed, we can see that almost any boat can be regarded as having a good turn of speed in the right conditions.

The recipe for speed

The basic ingredients required for speed are relatively simple. First of all, plenty of sail area and an efficient rig are required to provide a high driving force; secondly, low resistance must be achieved through a long waterline, light weight and low wetted surface area, together with an efficient hull shape, and a good keel for windward performance; finally, the boat must have sufficient stability so that the maximum possible amount of sail can be carried. The different ways in which these are combined, together with the extent of any sacrifices made for the interior layout or for seaworthiness, determine the boat's performance. Now let us look at the hull design in more detail.

Resistance

A number of factors affect the resistance of the boat to forward motion, and we shall examine each of them briefly in turn. To begin with, we shall look at the simple case of a boat sailing dead downwind. Here, there are two primary components of resistance: first of all, there is frictional resistance, due to water rubbing along the sides of the hull; secondly, there is wave-making resistance, caused by the hull creating a disturbance in the water and pushing up a train of waves. The frictional resistance is clearly minimised by keeping the wetted area of the hull to a minimum, which means deep, rounded hull sections, a fine stern, no bustle, and a small keel and rudder. A smooth bottom also reduces resistance, as may be expected.

Wave-making resistance is somewhat more complex, but the two basic factors are displacement and waterline length. The lower the displacement, the less water is pushed aside by the boat, and so the smaller the waves. The effect of waterline length is not quite as simple. Basically, the distance between bow and stern waves depends on the boat's speed; at a speed in knots of around $1.4\sqrt{LWL}$ in feet ($2.54\sqrt{LWL}$ in metres), the so-called maximum hull speed, the bow and stern waves become superimposed upon one another, and there is a marked increase in wave-making resistance. This increase is greatest with heavy-displacement boats, as the waves created are much larger than with a light boat.

The weight of a boat relative to her size is expressed by the displacement:length ratio (DLR), calculated thus:

$$DLR = \frac{D \text{ in tons}}{(0.01 LWL \text{ in feet})^3} \quad or \quad \frac{D \text{ in tonnes}}{(0.1 LWL \text{ in metres})^3}$$

A boat with a DLR in excess of 250 ton/cu. ft (9 t/cu.m) is unlikely to exceed its hull speed, no matter how much sail is carried. Boats with a DLR of 100 ton/cu. ft (3.5 t/cu. m) or less are light enough to pick up and plane off the wind, and so their maximum speed is really only limited by how well the crew can control them.

The split of resistance between frictional and wave-making components varies with the speed:length ratio (Speed in knots ÷√LWL). Taking a relatively heavy-displacement boat as an example, wave-making resistance is negligible up to a ratio of about 0.5. By the time the speed:length ratio has reached 1.1 the resistance is split equally between the two components, and at maximum hull speed wave-making resistance is over six times greater than the frictional resistance. On a lighter boat the wave-making resistance is proportionately less, particularly at higher boat speeds.

Another, often underestimated contributor to the boat's resistance is the propeller installation. The major factor here is the propeller itself if fixed, or the shafting if a folding propeller is fitted. If the boat is to have good performance under sail, a folding propeller is virtually essential, as a fixed propeller can easily take half a knot off the boat's speed. The best solution, from the sailing viewpoint, is an outboard motor that is raised out of the water when sailing. The effect of the propeller is greatest at low boat speeds, as at higher speeds it quickly becomes masked by the massive wave-making resistance.

If we now bring the boat onto the wind, additional sources of resistance arise. First of all the boat heels over. The asymmetry that this induces in the hull shape increases the wave-making resistance, but depending upon the hull form the wetted surface area may either increase or decrease. The angle of heel also results in a downward component in the force of the sails, pushing the boat deeper into the water, increasing its displacement and therefore its resistance.

Secondly, the hull has to counteract the sideways force of the sails, which can be several times greater than the propulsive force when close hauled. This is achieved by the keel and rudder – and to a much smaller extent the hull – which as the boat makes leeway create a lift force equal in magnitude to the rig's side force. In the process, a trail of

VOLVO PENTA
MD 11/120 S

Fig 2.1 *Volvo Penta MD11/120S saildrive unit. In addition to ease of installation, a saildrive has significantly less drag than a conventional propeller shaft and P-bracket.* (Photo Volvo Penta (UK) Ltd)

vortices streams behind the hull, keel and rudder, resulting in induced drag – typically one third of the total resistance when beating at full power. The pressure difference about the keel and rudder also produces an extra surface wave whenever the top of either foil comes near or passes through the water surface.

Stability

The term 'stability' is used in a rather loose way when it comes to yacht design. The interpretation that first comes to mind is the boat's stability at normal angles of heel in flat water conditions, when stability is balanced against the boat's sail area. However, the designer also needs to bear in mind numerous other facets of stability, such as the boat's stability at large angles of heel, behaviour in large seas and breaking waves, and the directional stability of the boat.

Stability in normal conditions is created solely by the moment between the boat's centre of gravity and the centre of volume of the immersed portion of the hull, the centre of buoyancy. There are, though, a number of techniques by which the designer can maximise this.

Firstly, the heavier the boat the greater the righting moment. Secondly, at normal angles of heel a flared hull form, with V-ed rather than U-shaped topsides, will quickly move the centre of buoyancy to leeward as the boat heels, giving a large righting lever. Unfortunately, though, once the deck edge is immersed the centre of buoyancy cannot move further to leeward, and stability is quickly lost. However, to some extent this can be offset through a large, high coachroof, which will improve the stability characteristics as it becomes immersed.

Another factor is the position of the centre of gravity: the lower it is, the further it swings up to weather as the boat heels. For a given set of scantlings, a heavy boat gains on two counts: first, simply through the extra weight; second, by the effect of moving more of the weight low down into the keel. A low centre of gravity makes a contribution to stability at all angles of heel, and so from the safety point of view it is to be preferred to a design with the same stability at small angles of heel, but which achieves it through a higher centre of gravity and more flared hull sections.

As well as moving the centre of gravity down, it can also be moved to weather by sitting the crew out on the rail. This is generally used on racing yachts as, so far as the rating rules are concerned, it is free stability. However, as the angle of heel increases the crew have an ever-diminishing effect on stability. So, even though a design may rely on crew weight for stability at moderate heel angles, the designer still needs to ensure that there is sufficient righting moment when well heeled or capsized.

The stability of a boat is often summarised by the righting moment curve (fig 2.3), which shows the righting moment at any given angle of heel. Until recently designers have generally just

looked at small-angle stability and relied on experience to assess the large-angle stability of the boat. However, as most reputable designers have access to a computer these days, a full set of stability curves can easily be drawn up, and hopefully more builders will supply these figures in their sales literature.

Looking at figure 2.3, a number of features can be picked out. First of all, stability falls off quite quickly with heel, reaching a maximum at about 60 degrees, and by about 120 degrees the boat has no more reserves of stability left. Thus, if heeled beyond this point the boat will remain stable in a capsized position, unless some external righting force is applied – for example, by a passing wave. The boat must be heeled back to about 120 degrees for her to right herself. Between 60 and 90 degrees of heel the effects of the coachroof can be seen, adding quite a large amount to the boat's reserves of stability.

Whilst the righting moment shows the actual force available

Fig 2.2 *Small, light boats are less stable than larger ones, as is clearly shown by the ease with which this J-24 was pulled over for a scrub.* (Photo Jo Aldridge)

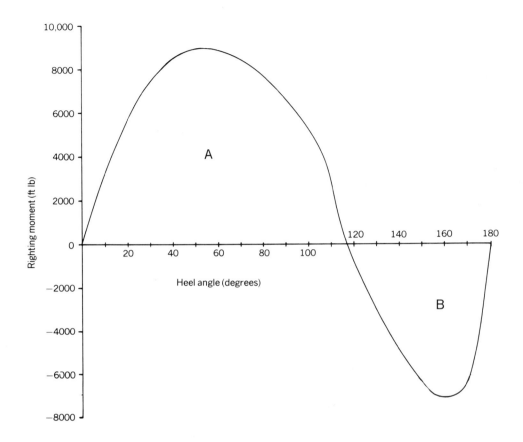

Fig 2.3 *Righting moment curve of a typical 26 ft (7.9 m) yacht. The ratio between the areas* A *and* B *is a measure of her seaworthiness.*

to right the boat in any given conditions of heel, the area between the curve and the horizontal axis indicates the total work required to heel the boat from one point on the curve to another: the greater the area, the more stable the boat will be when hit by a gust of wind or a wave. Thus, the ratios of the total areas enclosed by the curve above (A) and below (B) the axis give an indication of the ultimate reserves of stability of the boat: if there is a much greater area above the axis than below, more work will be needed to capsize her and less work to bring her upright again.

In addition to the righting curve, the other factor affecting a boat's behaviour when heeled is the balance between the bow and stern sections.

The fuller the stern is in relation to the bows, the more the boat will trim down by the bows as she heels. This can be seen *in extremis* when an IOR-style yacht is pinned down on her ear with spinnaker up, bows dug in and stern well up in the air. As this happens, the rudder rises out of the water and the helmsman quickly loses control over the boat when he needs it most. The only way out is to free off all the sails and let the boat rise in her own time. Furthermore, if the bows are too deep in profile the boat can develop a lot of weather helm as she heels, due to the forefoot digging in and moving the centre of resistance well forwards. A boat with flatter sections and a more raised forefoot will gain dynamic lift to raise the bows, so long as she has way on.

Stability in waves

So far we have only really looked at the need for stability in flat water conditions. However, stability in waves is particularly important in small boats, as the wave size is proportionately much greater for a small boat than a large one, and so the possibility of a wave-induced capsize or knockdown is that much greater.

Here the model is much more complex than in the flat water case as, in addition to studying the geometry of the boat, the behaviour of the sail plan and the size and shape of the waves must be considered, and the whole system regarded as a dynamic one instead of a much simpler static system. Thus, although I will not attempt to go into great detail, the effects of a number of design features can be picked out.

The first thing to realise is that a wide, shallow hull will fit the contour of the face of a wave, causing the boat to heel quite considerably as the wave passes and losing an appreciable amount of stability. On the other hand, a slender hull with a low centre of gravity and a deeper, longer keel will stay more upright due to the pendulum effect of the low centre of gravity and the large area of keel immersed in the deeper, stiller waters, damping down the motion.

As the boat goes over the wave crest, she is floating temporarily higher out of the water, and even more stability is lost, making the boat particularly prone to capsize by a breaking wave crest. Thus, due to this 'contouring' to the waves boats that have more than adequate stability in flat water may be quite different in rough seas. This tallies with sailing experience, as in windy conditions it is ultimately the sea state and not the wind strength that determines how hard one can drive the boat. Lastly, the beamier the boat, the greater the area of hull presented to a breaking wavecrest, and so the greater the chance of the boat capsizing if caught beam-on to a sea. This effect is much greater than the increase in stability at moderate heel angles that is gained through the wider beam.

To counteract these destabilising tendencies, the motion must be damped, in much the same way as shock absorbers damp the motion of a car over a bumpy road. One damping mechanism common to all vessels is their underwater body, with a long, deep keel being a great asset. A keel with a large stall-angle performs best, so low aspect-ratio keels or bilge keels are an advantage. In a similar way, the sails can be a great roll-damper, as illustrated by the large number of motor fishing vessels that still carry steadying sails. However, this form of damping is largely restricted to sailing on the wind and reaching, as when the apparent wind angle moves aft of about 120 degrees the rig becomes dynamically unstable and can increase the boat's rolling motion instead. Thus a sailing boat's motion is very steady on the wind, but on a run she can roll heavily if the sea state and hull design permit. Another important consideration is the way the weight is distributed in the boat: when the weight is positioned in the ends of the boat, away from the centre of gravity, a lot more energy is absorbed by the boat. In the same way, if a boat is dismasted her motion immediately becomes much more severe, as the rig is by far the largest factor in the boat's weight distribution.

The shape of the ends of the boat have a dramatic effect on her seaworthiness. First of all, the bows need to have enough buoyancy so that they lift to any oncoming wave, either through well flared sections, or a bow that sweeps well up in profile, with flat sections underneath. A deep forefoot with insufficient flare, as was once prevalent in the IOR, just digs into the wave, moves the centre of resistance well forward and upsets the balance of the boat – often to such an extent that a broach is inevitable. Similarly, although a wide flat stern can promote surfing and reduce wave-making resistance, if carried to excess it means that the rudder lifts out of the water as the boat heels and the helmsman loses control.

Two factors have not yet been touched upon, namely the actions of the crew and the waters in which the boat sails. Although it is irrefutable that the older, deeper, narrower, and heavier designs are much more seaworthy in extreme conditions, the behaviour of the crew can make any boat unseaworthy, or make a boat survive a storm in conditions under which she could not look after herself. Keeping enough sail on to keep good steerage way on the boat and ensuring that the boat meets the waves correctly, probably do more than anything else to make a boat seaworthy. However, it does demand a great deal of effort from the crew, together with an adequate depth of experience.

Furthermore, when selecting a design the question one should ask oneself is not 'Is it absolutely seaworthy?' – for I doubt if such a vessel exists – but 'Is it sufficiently seaworthy for my planned use of the boat?'. Thus, an experienced racing crew will probably have more reserves of energy and experience than the average owner and so will be able to sail a less seaworthy boat. Also, if the boat is being used solely for short, sheltered coastal trips she is bound to experience much less severe conditions than, say, a boat crossing the Atlantic. Boats sailing in well sheltered waters, such as the Solent, are extremely unlikely to be capsized by a breaking wave. However, they must still have sufficient reserves of stability to recover from a knockdown (see fig 2.4).

Keel design

Keels have fascinated designers and owners ever since the resurgence of the fin keel in modern designs. No doubt, part of this interest has been due to the keel being virtually a separate entity from the hull, enabling the owner to assess its shape easily and the designer to play around with different keel designs at a relatively modest cost. Another factor is the analogy between a keel and an aircraft's wing, meaning that designers have had access to a large amount of design data on the subject. Finally, the wing keel developments in 12-metres (largely devised to increase the efficiency of a low-draft keel

Fig 2.4 *A lightweight design is great fun to sail in sheltered waters, but a capsize is always a possibility when she is driven hard.*
(Photo Jo Aldridge)

and to help get the lead down low), with all the publicity created by their contribution to the America's Cup competition, have brought the keel to the forefront of the yachtsman's mind.

Let us look at what the aircraft designers can teach us about foil design. First, the keel needs to be as deep as possible to minimise the induced drag, by reducing the amount of water that flows round from the high- to the low-pressure side. Second, the keel needs to be nearly upright and with considerably less taper than most keels have nowadays. There is an advantage in the elliptical profile used by many designers, but it is very small. The actual section needs to be as thin as possible to minimise drag, with a moderately full entry to delay stalling, but the point of maximum fullness fairly well aft.

But how good is this analogy between aircraft and yachts? Clearly the same basic laws of fluid dynamics apply, but there are several additional factors that are not generally taken into account sufficiently. Firstly, the keel works close to the surface of the water and so the flow is modified by pressure differences, causing surface waves which then interact with the hull waves to affect the boat's wave-making resistance. Secondly, the conditions under which an aerofoil operates are generally much more stable than those found when sailing; both the boat's pitching and rolling, and the motion of water particles in the waves mean that the keel is generally operating in rapidly fluctuating water speeds and flow directions. Finally, the keel also has to have sufficient volume to carry enough ballast low down to give the boat stability. This often results in keels that are fatter at the bottom than at the top, whilst an aircraft wing's strength requirements demand that the wing is thickest at the root, right beside the fuselage. In addition, there is generally a draft restriction, either imposed by the rating rules or simply by the depth of water in which the boat sails.

The wave-making effect of the keel is least harmful when it is either spread along a considerable length of the hull by raking the keel aft, or when the keel is kept below the water as far as possible, by cutting away the top of the keel or using an 'upside-down' keel that is longer at the bottom than at the top. The effect of the unsteady water flow over the keel can be countered to some extent by using a fatter, more stall-resistant section, especially near the tip where the effect is greatest. A low aspect ratio foil also helps, as its length effectively counters the fluctuations in water flow. Alternatively, the keel can be fitted with wings, which stabilise the water flow round the tip and also damp some of the boat's motion. At the top of the keel, extra length helps to keep the flow of water attached to it.

The requirement for a low centre of gravity in the keel can be met in several ways: on a conventional keel the length and the thickness can be increased towards the tip, enabling the weight to be moved down; a fuller-section shape can be used, enabling the weight to be lowered without fattening the keel unduly; a bulb or wings can be fitted. A good combination in this last case is a cast-iron keel that is relatively light and cheap, with lead wings or bulb on the bottom, using the extra density of the lead to keep weight low down without increasing the drag unnecessarily. Note that there is no stability gain inherent in simply fitting a lead keel as opposed to an iron one, though if they have the same profile area then the lead one will be slightly slimmer and thus have less resistance.

Steering arrangements

On a small boat tiller steering is the natural choice, except on a motor sailer with an interior steering position or where some other unusual requirements must be met. It has the advantages of taking up little room, being cheap and simple to install, and responsive. The rudder may be mounted on the transom or underneath the hull. The latter makes the boat look more like a small yacht and sacrifices some room in the cockpit by moving the helmsman further forward. A transom-mounted rudder is simpler to install and maintain, although it is perhaps slightly less efficient. It also has the advantage of being removable when the boat is trailed or berthed on mud.

As with most aspects of yacht design, the requirements of rudder design are somewhat contradictory. The blade needs to be as deep as possible so that the maximum area remains immersed as the boat heels, especially on boats with wide, full sterns; on the other hand, a low aspect-ratio blade will have a larger stalling angle and so will give a larger maximum steering force. Clearly, the rudder needs to be large enough to provide an adequate steering force; on the other hand, windward performance is more efficient if the boat has a large keel and smaller rudder, as the rudder is less efficient at counteracting leeway due to its working in the disturbed wake of the keel. Positioning the stock further back along the blade means that less force is required to steer the boat, but at the cost of less 'feel' for the helmsman.

In addition to providing a steering force, the rudder acts as a stabiliser, making the boat more likely to travel in a straight line. This requirement is particularly important in waves, as the combination of the varying water motion of the different parts of the waves and the forces developed by the boat's motion means that there is little tendency otherwise for the boat to steer in a straight line. Here length in both the keel and rudder is a great help, as the water takes longer to change its flow pattern round the foil and so the disruptive forces are effectively damped out.

The ultimate answer here is a deep forefoot and full-length keel, with the rudder mounted on the trailing edge of the keel. In an effort to reduce wetted surface area, however, designers cut away the leading and trailing edges of the keel, and the resultant profile was not sufficiently stabilising to sail in a straight line. In response, the rudder was separated from the keel and moved to the stern. Adding a deep skeg (not the shallow IOR-style appendage, which is there purely for rating reasons) in front of the blade once again increases its length and makes the boat directionally more stable, at the cost of slightly more drag and less responsive handling. An additional bonus is that the skeg both strengthens and protects the rudder blade.

Emergency steering

Whilst this is a frequent topic for articles in sailing magazines, I am afraid that I have yet to come across a really effective form of emergency steering to cope with rudder failures. The favourite, accepted by the ORC for IOR yachts, is to tie a floorboard to the end of a spinnaker pole, and attach this to the transom for use as a giant steering oar. Another approach is to use a strong bucket, or something else with plenty of drag, and trail it behind the boat on a bight of rope, pulling it round to the side that you want to steer towards. This works better if the rope can be poled out to move the bucket further outboard. These devices can be counted on to steer the boat between a fetch and a broad reach, so long as the boat is not carrying too much sail and the sails are trimmed to balance the boat well. However they are unlikely to be efficient enough for the boat to be able to sail to windward in order to get out of trouble.

The other source of steering problems lies in the tiller, particularly on boats that use a relatively lightweight metal tiller. A spare tiller should be carried if you have any doubts about the one fitted. Furthermore, you should ensure that removing the tiller does not permit the rudder to drop out of the bottom of the boat, as has been known to happen.

Factors of safety

There are several ways in which a yacht can come to grief, but a lot can be done to minimise the danger, if the boat has been designed with sufficient forethought. As in all other areas of yachting, a compromise must be reached to suit the use to which the boat will be put, as all safety features both add to the cost of the vessel and detract from other design factors.

As we have seen, yachts are not immune from capsizing,

given suitable weather conditions. Whether the boat is just knocked down onto her beam ends or is rolled right over, the main problem is water penetrating into the boat's interior, as this reduces both the amount of buoyancy and the boat's stability. Whilst most boats can easily remain afloat with 18 inches (45 centimetres) or so of water in the bilges in calm conditions, in a rough sea the effect of all this water slopping around will be to make the boat so tender that she may be rolled several times by the waves until she fills up completely and sinks.

The first point is to ensure that the boat can be made completely watertight by sealing all hatches and locker lids, also ensuring that they are strong enough for the job. Problems often occur when a foredeck hatch blows open under the pressure of water, or when a crew member accidentally kicks open a cockpit locker climbing up to weather in a broach. The effects of this can be minimised by ensuring that the cockpit lockers do not open directly into the interior of the boat. Ideally they should have their own pumping arrangement – either a separate pump or a hose T-ed into the main system.

Another step towards safety is to incorporate boyancy in the hull to prevent the boat sinking. An increasing number of production boats fill the space between the main hull and the inner moulding with sufficient foam to achieve this, and if carefully planned the loss in usable space is minimal. This buoyancy needs to be carefully distributed both fore-and-aft and athwartships, to ensure that the boat is stable in the flooded condition. Alternatively, inflatable bags can be fitted which can be rapidly inflated by a gas bottle in times of need. If the boat is fitted with adequate buoyancy it can be argued that a liferaft is no longer necessary, at least for coastal and inshore passages.

Built-in buoyancy is obviously also very useful if the boat's hull is holed and she starts sinking, not so much if she has been driven ashore, but more if the boat strikes an offshore rock or is involved in a collision. Another safety feature is a double bottom, as is found in many ships and in 'trailer sailers' with water ballast carried under the cabin sole, since in this case two structural layers have to be breached before the water comes in.

Regarding the rig, if the boat should capsize, the drag of the mast and sails under water may well prove sufficient to prevent the boat being rolled upright by another wave. So in this one situation a weak link in the rig may prove to be an advantage. However, once the boat is righted, the absence of the damping effect of the rig will cause the boat to roll more, and she may capsize again as a result. Furthermore, a mast falling down and sliding about the boat may easily punch a hole in the hull or injure a crewman. In addition to the above-deck part of the mast being a danger, the lower portion of a broken keel-stepped mast could also come loose and be thrown round the cabin, so the mast heel should be properly secured to the mast step or hull structure. In a similar way, all loose items down below – anchors, batteries, cooker, locker lids, etc. – should be able to be properly secured. It is not very pleasant waking up in a shower of floorboards and tins of food if the boat should be knocked down when you are off watch!

Fig 2.5 *After a dismasting, the first task is to recover or jettison the remains of the rig.* (Photo Jo Aldridge)

The engine and propeller

Today virtually all yachts carry some form of engine, even if only a small outboard motor, partly because owners and crew have to be able to ensure that they return from a voyage in time, and partly because of the tight manoeuvring often required to get on and off moorings, or in and out of a marina berth.

To choose an engine of the right size, one should aim somewhere between one and three horsepower per thousand pounds (450 kilos) displacement. The lower figure will really only be suitable for use when coming alongside or when becalmed, whereas the higher figure will effectively make the boat into a motor sailer, able to motor effectively in the worst of conditions. When selecting an engine, one should look at the engine's maximum rpm, in addition to the horsepower produced. This is because a slower turning engine will tend to be more reliable, due to the lower level of stress, and its lower-pitched noise will be less obtrusive. These benefits must be balanced against the smaller size, lighter weight and lower initial cost of a high-revving engine.

The simplest form of installation is an outboard motor, either clamped onto a bracket on the transom or housed in a well in the cockpit, from which it can easily be lowered down into the water. Its advantages are that it is cheap and simple, and takes up no room inside the boat. Furthermore, if it fails then one can easily put it in the car boot at the end of the day and take it away for repair.

Unfortunately, because of the shallow depth of the propeller on an outboard, it can easily come out of the water when conditions are rough or when motor-sailing (most outboards are limited to a choice of 15- or 20-in (38 or 51 cm) shaft lengths. Furthermore, if the motor is mounted on the transom it can be quite hard work manhandling it on and off the mounting bracket (a 5-hp engine typically weighs about 45 lb (20 kg), rising to some 80 lb (36 kg) for a 10-hp engine. It is basically the sheer weight of the outboard motor that restricts its use on larger boats.

Most outboard motor engines have been developed from motorcycle engine technology, and so they tend to be high-revving two-stroke engines. Four-stroke units are also available and they tend to be much more economical on fuel, though the penalty for this is that they are generally 10 – 20 lb (5 – 9 kg) heavier.

If the outboard is mounted on a bracket on the transom, this should slide up on a track or be hinged, both to keep the shaft out of the water when sailing and to bring it up to a more convenient height for starting and for mounting. The alternative is to have the outboard mounted in a well in the cockpit. This is generally a permanent stowage for the outboard, enabling a more powerful engine to be used than would otherwise be the case. Furthermore, the further forward the well is located, the less chance there is of the propeller coming too close to the water's surface. Under sail, the outboard is raised by a rope tackle, and a blanking piece is generally supplied to avoid any disturbance to the water flow. With this type of installation it is important that the well is properly ventilated, as otherwise petrol fumes can form an explosive mixture with the air.

On larger boats an inboard engine will probably be fitted, giving better performance under power, plus the advantage of being able to recharge the batteries without going ashore. The penalty is that the engine alone is at least twice as heavy as an outboard of equivalent power, without taking into account the weight of the engine bearers, shaft, propeller, fuel and cooling systems. In addition, the shaft and propeller add considerably to the boat's resistance, particularly in light airs.

To minimise this drag, the shaft should be as short and, more importantly, as near horizontal as possible. A fixed propeller also makes a major contribution to drag, at least as great as the rest of the installation (the difference in performance between a folding and a fixed two-bladed propeller easily amounts to half a knot or more). As sailing yachts are generally not capable of being driven at high speed under power, there is generally little advantage to be had from a fixed propeller when weighed against the better performance under sail with a folding propeller. However, in reverse a folding propeller is less efficient, because the blades are only held open by centrifugal force. To ensure that the blades open and close correctly, they should be geared together in the hub, so the weight of one blade prevents the other from flopping open when the boat is under sail. The feathering propeller seen on

VOLVO PENTA
MD 17D/MS 2

Fig 2.6 *Volvo Penta* MD17D/
MS2 *marine diesel engine.*
(Photo Volvo Penta (UK) Ltd)

IOR boats is purely a rating dodge and would not be fitted were it not for a loophole in the rule. They are at least twice the cost of a folding propeller, and the extended blades are more likely to catch weed or plastic bags.

Selecting the right size of propeller is a complex task, and in general the easiest solution is to ask the engine manufacturer for his recommendations. On the design side, the relevant factors are the engine power and speed, the designed speed of the vessel and, to some extent, the shape of the stern. For a racing boat, the rating rule will probably have a great influence on the choice of propeller diameter. And from a practical point of view there needs to be adequate clearance between the propeller tips and the hull – at least 10 per cent of the propeller diameter, and preferably 15 to 20 per cent. Once installed, if the engine cannot achieve maximum revs, the propeller is too large or has too much pitch; if the engine easily reaches maximum speed and yet the boat's performance is poor, a larger propeller or one with greater pitch should be fitted. Generally a slow-turning, large-diameter propeller will have more thrust to drive the boat in bad weather, whereas a rapidly spinning small propeller will give a higher maximum speed in calm waters.

The installation of an inboard engine is more or less standardised on boats of this size: the engine is flexibly mounted to minimise noise and vibration, and the shaft is rigidly connected to the gearbox, passing through a flexibly mounted stern gland, with a rubber cutless bearing in the bracket. Thus, the entire drive train has only two points at which it can move – the engine mounts and the P-bracket

Fig 2.7 *Although a deep propeller is more efficient, the only reason for the shaft to pass through the keel is to improve a boat's IOR rating.*

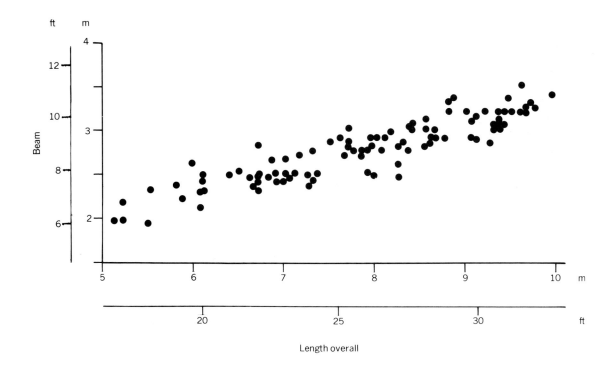

Fig 2.8 *Length overall* (LOA) *v*
beam.

bearing. The alternative is to use a rigid bearing on the shaft, and a flexible coupling to attach the shaft to the gearbox, allowing movement at the coupling and the engine mounts. The rigid bearing on the shaft may be required simply to prevent a long shaft flexing excessively. Alternatively, the flexible coupling may be introduced to break the shaft and alter the shaft line, enabling it to run more horizontally inside the boat and reducing the angle at which the engine is mounted. On no account should there be either more or less than two flexible points in the system.

Design parameters

In order to assess a given design, we must first of all know where the boat stands in relation to other designs, and how all the different design parameters interact. To do this, I have plotted graphs showing data for all boats up to about 33 ft (10

m) available in Britain at the time of writing. Some of these are old designs or replicas of older craft, so the survey effectively covers the whole range of design, not just modern practice.

Taking the length:beam ratio first, from the graph (fig. 2.8) we can see that smaller boats are beamier in relation to their length compared to larger designs. This is the case for a number of reasons: first, a beamier boat gives quite a lot more room on board; second, the smaller boats are less likely to sail in exposed waters and so can safely be designed with a beamier hull, despite its worse performance in waves; third, a small boat is more reliant on crew weight for stability, as the crew represents a much higher proportion of the boat's total ballast and, in addition the centre of gravity tends to be higher due to small boats generally being lighter.

One factor that limits the beam on many boats is the

Fig 2.9 *Displacement:length ratio (DLR) v waterline length (LWL).*

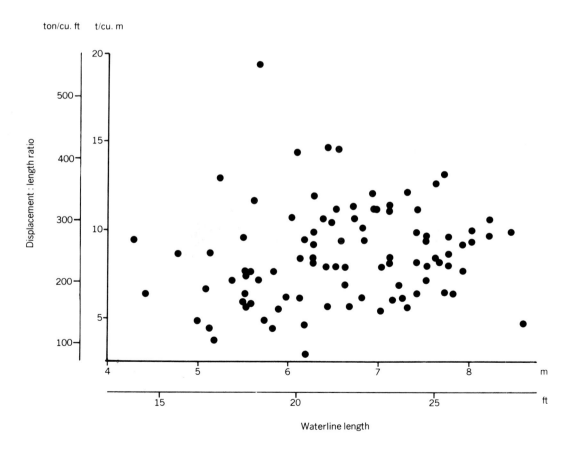

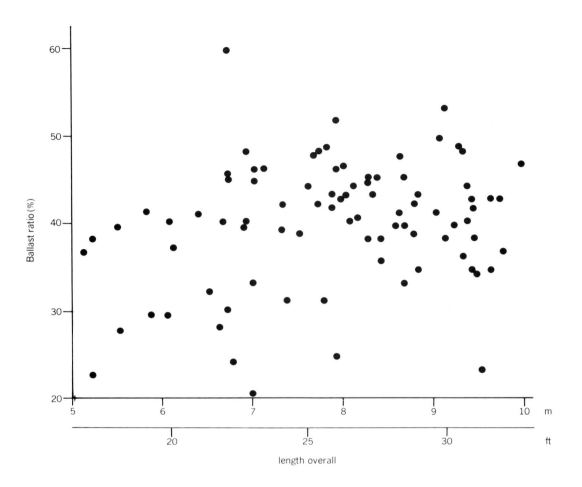

Fig 2.10 *Ballast ratio (% of displacement) v length overall (LOA).*

maximum width which can legally be trailed behind a car – 8 ft 2 in (2.5 m) in the EEC. As can be seen on the chart, boats up to 29 ft (9 m) in length are designed to this beam restriction, and then there is a jump in beam, due to many boats having been squeezed to fit inside the limit.

Now let us turn to the other major hull design parameter, the boat's displacement. As we have seen in the section on resistance, the weight of a boat in respect to her size is best expressed by the displacement:length ratio (DLR), and so this is the parameter plotted.

There is quite a large scatter in this plot (Fig 2.9), ranging from lightweight racing designs with a DLR of 110 – 200 tons/ cu. ft (4 – 7 t/cu. m) to really heavy boats with a DLR well above the design averages. The first thing to notice, though, is that the longer boats tend to have a higher DLR. This is because they need to be built more strongly and they also tend to have a better fitted out interior. Furthermore, the fact that the boats are heavier means that the crew's weight – whether perched on the rail or just sitting in the cockpit – increases the boat's stability by a lesser amount, and this results in the boat needing to be still heavier in compensation. This can lead to a vicious circle unless the designer reaches a compromise somewhere along the line. Also, many of the smaller boats are

Fig 2.11 *Ballast ratio (% of displacement) v displacement:length ratio (DLR).*

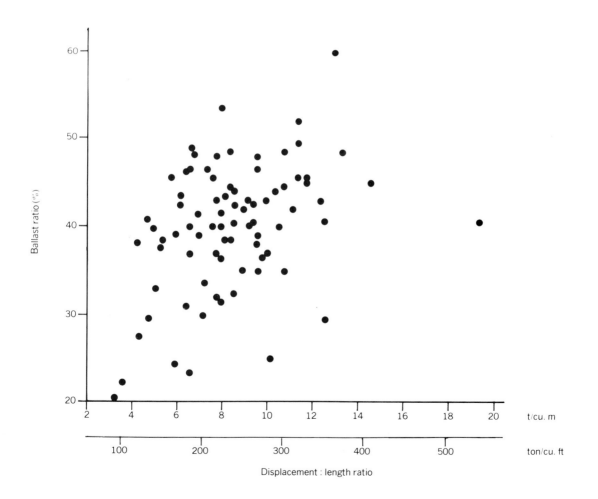

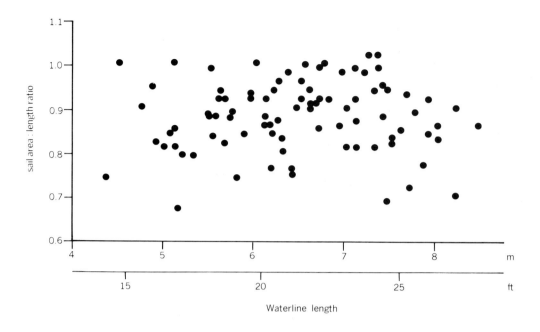

Waterline length

Fig 2.12 ✓ Sail area:length ratio v
waterline length (LWL).

designed to be towed by road, and the heavier they are, the
larger the car required to pull them along.

As a rough and ready guide, a moderate displacement boat
will have a DLR at least as great as her waterline length in
metric units. Ultra-light boats with a DLR approaching half this
value have been built, though they are either very tender or
short of sail as a result. Boats with twice the average DLR have
also been built: their weight precludes any likelihood of a
good performance under sail, so they tend to be motor sailers
with a large engine and a voluminous, well-appointed interior.

Moving on to the other ratios (fig 2.10–2.15), these have been
plotted both against the boat's length and against her DLR,
which are effectively two different ways of determining her size
(a high DLR means high wave-making resistance, in just the
same way as a long boat will have high resistance due to a large
wetted surface area).

Although the ballast ratio is not a direct measure of a boat's
stability, it is a good pointer, at least to large-angle stability.
Looking at figure 2.10, we can see that the smaller boats have
a lower ballast ratio, due to their lighter displacement. This
varies from 20 per cent for what is basically a ballasted dinghy

with a lid, up to 40 per cent for a heavier-displacement boat more suited to sailing in exposed waters. The same trend can be seen in the plot against the DLR (fig 2.11), with the heavier boats having a higher ballast ratio, as the all-up weight of the boat is increasing at a faster rate than the weight of the structure, interior and rig.

If we now consider the sail area, the first ratio to look at is the ratio of the square root of the sail area to waterline length (fig 2.12 and 2.13). (The actual sail area of mainsail and largest genoa is used, instead of the foretriangle area, as otherwise the smaller overlapping area of a fractional boat's genoa makes her seem under-canvassed.) The sail area: length ratio approximates to the sail area:wetted surface area ratio, and so it is a guide to the boat's light airs performance. From figure 2.12, it is clear that under these conditions smaller boats are at no disadvantage. However, using this ratio alone assumes that boats have a similar hull form. But a heavier boat's fuller sections, for example, result in a larger wetted surface area, as does a long keel, and neither of these factors are reflected in the sail area:length ratio.

For good light airs performance, a boat generally needs a

Fig 2.13 √Sail area:length ratio v displacement:length ratio (DLR).

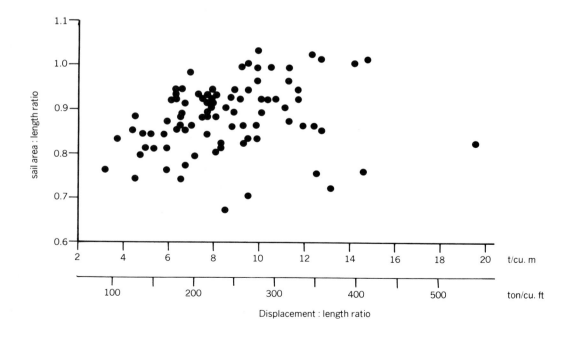

sail area:length ratio above 0.90, and ideally above 0.95. Anything above 1.0, and the boat may be biased too much towards light airs performance without the stability to carry the sails in a breeze; anything much below 0.85, and the boat will probably need to use her engine in light airs. However, as I have said, the lighter boats tend to have a smaller wetted surface area, and so the low sail area:length ratios of the boats with a low DLR (see fig 2.13) are not as disastrous as they may at first appear.

If we now move on to performance at higher speed:length ratios, say above 1.0, we need to use the sail area:displacement ratio. From both figures 2.14 and 2.15, it can be seen that the smaller, lighter boats have higher sail area:displacement ratios, and this explains their higher performance potential (stability and crew ability permitting).

Fig 2.14 *Sail area:displacement ratio v waterline length* (LWL).

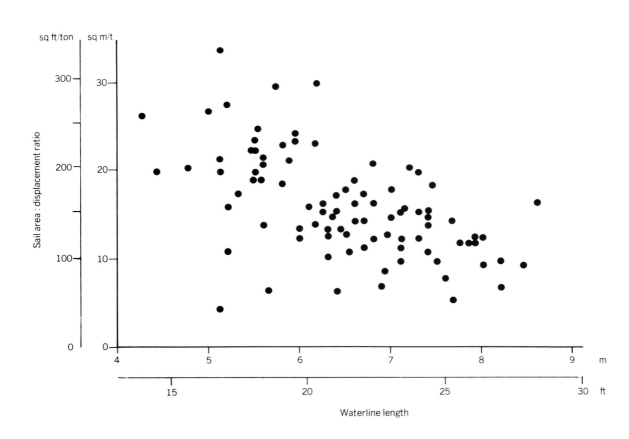

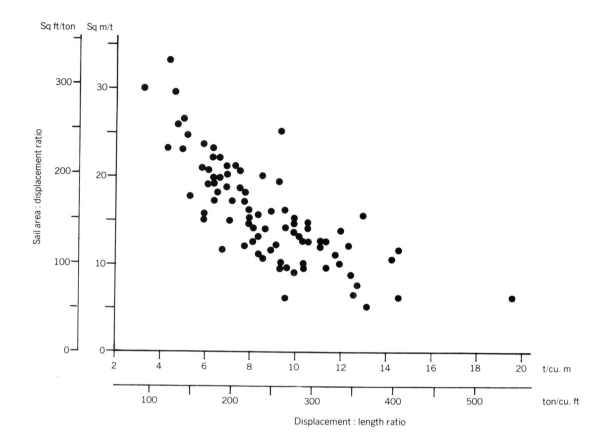

Fig 2.15 *Sail area:displacement ratio v displacement:length ratio (DLR).*

The reason that they get away with this is purely their greater reserves of stability. The plots also explain why smaller boats can be so hard to shake off downwind – their higher sail area:displacement ratios mean that in a given wind speed they tend to sail at higher speed:length ratios than larger boats.

Problems of scale

It is difficult to compare two boat's potential performance directly, as there is no simple correlation between sail area, length, displacement, stability and speed. However it is interesting to see how these factors 'scale' between one size of boat and another.

If we use the waterline length as our measure of size, then, for any given displacement:length ratio, the sail area will have to increase with the cube of the difference in length to keep the same ratio of sail area to wave-making resistance, and so maintain the same maximum speed:length ratio. Moreover, the sail area will have to increase with the square of the difference in length to maintain the same sail area:wetted surface area ratio, for light airs performance. Thus, if stability was no problem, the big boats would have sail area increased in proportion to the cube of waterline length, giving the same speed:length ratio in windy conditions, and enhanced performance in light airs.

Unfortunately stability is a problem: if we simply double the size of the boat and rig, stability is reduced. This means that larger boats are relatively undercanvassed, and so in a given wind strength will sail at a lower speed:length ratio. The only time when they come into their own is when the wind strength is such that smaller boats have reached their maximum speed while bigger boats have not, as a bigger boat needs a stronger wind to attain its maximum speed than a smaller one.

To counteract this, larger boats tend to be designed to a lower displacement:length ratio than smaller ones, partly due to the boat's structure being lighter than on a smaller boat. This same factor enables more weight to be placed in the keel, helping her gain much-needed stability. This helps in two ways: first, the lower displacement reduces the wave-making resistance, for heavy weather performance; second, it means that the boat can be designed with less wetted surface area, for light airs performance.

Hull construction

As we have seen, the vast majority of boats are now GRP production models. GRP construction is very different from timber or metal construction, as the actual strength of the material is determined by the skill of the laminator when he lays up the hull and the quality and environmental control at the factory, as well as by the properties of the materials that go into the laminate. This means that the designer has to allow for a much wider variation in the characteristics of the building material, compared to timber or metal where the properties are largely determined by the grade of metal or species of timber specified.

The advantages of GRP construction are that it is well suited to a marine environment due to the lack of corrosion problems (though osmosis can occur if poor materials are used or the workmanship is poor), and it is very resistant to minor damage such as dents and scrapes. The weight of a standard solid laminate with polyester resin and glass fibres is typically half that of steel and only slightly heavier than light alloy, and the use of sandwich construction, epoxy resin and Kevlar or carbon fibre reduces this markedly. Initial cost for a basic laminate is about 50 per cent higher than steel and 25 per cent lower than light alloy, and the subsequent maintenance costs are also very low. Furthermore, in the size of boat we are concerned with, the plating thickness on alloy boats becomes excessively thin if selected purely on a structural basis, leaving little in reserve to resist corrosion or provide good panel stiffness against collisions. So any metal boat must be considerably heavier than a plastic one.

The only material not considered so far is timber. Although the cost of timber is low, the high labour costs mean that it is relatively expensive for production boats. However, it is ideal for one-off boats in this size range, since the production costs of a one-off GRP boat are much higher than when a series of boats are being built. As far as weight is concerned, timber is generally slightly lighter than a standard production plastic laminate, though not quite as light as the most exotic laminates used in racing yachts.

An important consideration is that of matching the strength of the boat and all its components to the expected loadings. No matter how heavily built, an indestructible boat is impossible to produce. What is needed is for the designer to carefully assess the loads to which the hull and fittings will be subjected, weighing up the effects of the size and weight of the boat, whether it is for racing or cruising, and whether the design is for day sailing in sheltered waters or extended ocean voyages. The more exposed are the waters the boat is intended for, the larger and heavier the boat, and the larger the loads that the hull will be subjected to. Furthermore, as racing yachtsmen are greatly concerned with saving weight and they generally have a bigger budget for maintaining the boat, it is fair to assume that factors of safety can be lowered due to a higher standard of maintenance on racing craft, provided it is combined with a greater awareness by the crew of possible weaknesses.

GRP construction materials
The standard materials in a GRP laminate are polyester resin and 'E' glass, either in the form of chopped strand mat, which consists of a thin blanket of short fibres bonded together, or in rovings, which are made into a fairly loosely woven cloth of fibres. Epoxy resin is superior to polyester due to much lower shrinkage on curing, improved bonding strength, proof against osmosis, and its being much less brittle than polyester. But the price for these improved properties is almost double that of polyester resin.

There are, in fact, two basic types of polyester resin – orthophthalic and isophthalic. The isophthalic resins are to be preferred, both because of their better structural properties and, perhaps more importantly, because of their better water resistance, and so resistance against osmosis. Thus even if costs preclude the use of orthophthalic resins throughout the boat, their use should at least be considered in the gelcoat of the hull moulding.

On the fibre side, the first alternative is 'R' glass (also called 'S' glass) which is a higher grade of glass than 'E', with improved stiffness and strength characteristics. Another alternative is Kevlar, which is lighter than glass, much stronger in tension and more resistant against impact loads. For this reason it is sometimes used in the bows of the lighter, more performance-orientated production boats, as well as having become the fibre normally used in racing yachts. However, while du Pont retain a monopoly over its manufacture, costs will remain relatively high, about four times the cost of 'E' glass. Finally, there is carbon fibre, which is very strong and stiff, but also brittle and poor in torsion. Its high cost (around ten times greater than 'E' glass on a weight-for-weight basis) restricts its use almost entirely to racing yachts, though it is also used to produce unstayed masts, where there is a great need for rigidity.

The big problem with GRP is its flexibility (this is why it is used for sail battens, and is also one of the reasons why it cannot be used for structural purposes in large ships). To try and overcome this, sandwich construction is often used, whereby a lightweight core effectively increases the thickness of the structure, and thus its strength and stiffness, with little increase in weight or cost. When the panel bends, one skin is put in tension and the other goes in compression, and the core takes the transverse compression and shear loads. End-grain balsa is the standard core material for production use, though the relatively high weight of the material and the large amount of resin it soaks up during construction mean that it is not often used in racing yachts. These will generally use lighter PVC foam, though paper, Nomex or plastic honeycomb are being used increasingly despite the problems in achieving a good bond to the laminate.

In fact, the quality of the bond between the laminate and the core is the key to any successful sandwich construction, as the glue line must take very high localised loads. In the long term, polyester resin has failed here, and more flexible, more durable specialised bonding pastes have been developed. The superior properties of epoxy resin avoid this problem, except with honeycomb cores, especially in large structures, where getting a reliable bond is difficult. Whatever materials are used, the bond can be much improved by vacuum-bagging the core and laminates while curing. This applies a high, even pressure over the entire laminate, and so ensures better bonding between the layers, and reduced likelihood of voids in the laminate.

As well as the actual materials used, the way in which the laminate is put together is also important. This is because, though a more resin-rich laminate is more weather resistant, a laminate with less resin is much stronger and stiffer, due to the fibres having better structural properties than the resin, whose primary purpose is simply to bond together and stabilise the fibres. The lowest structural properties are found in laminates which are sprayed on, or those which contain just chopped strand mat, as both laminates are rich in resin, and the short fibres do not distribute the loads throughout the structure well. Next come a wide range of cloths and woven rovings. The thinner a cloth is for a given weight, the less resin it will use and the stronger the resulting laminate. A closely woven cloth will also have greater resistance to sharp impacts. Moreover, the weave determines how easily the cloth will drape to the complex curvature of the mould. Finally, there are the uni-directional materials, consisting of a broad tape in which all the fibres go in one direction, giving a very thin laminate using very little resin. It also permits the designer to specify the fibre orientation for optimum structural characteristics.

GRP construction techniques

The actual techniques used in plastic construction vary from those used by a yard building a one-off design, through those used for small runs to a particular design in a small yard, to the production-line approach of the large boatbuilding factories.

In a large factory the floor space will be divided up into a number of separate 'shops' for laminating up the hull and deck, manufacturing the internal mouldings, prefabricating the interior joinery, and fitting out the boat. In addition, there will be storage areas, areas for mixing the resins, etc. The various components will be moved round the factory on cradles or by overhead cranes.

The laminating shops will have a carefully maintained environment, with control of both the temperature and humidity to give the optimum curing conditions, and of the styrene content in the air (emitted by the curing polyester resin) to preserve the health of the workers. The components may be laminated by a spray gun fed with polyester resin and continuous glass fibres, which are chopped into short lengths as they are mixed with the resin and sprayed onto the hull. Alternatively, the hull may be laminated manually, which increases labour costs, but enables higher-quality woven rovings to be used in the laminate, in combination with chopped strand mat. For small mouldings, injection moulding techniques may be used, or a pair of matched moulds used to ensure that the moulding has a good finish on both sides.

For the fittings and interior joinery, components can be cut out and machined by fully automated tools, either on site or by a sub-contractor. The bulk of the joinery will be assembled off the boat and should not need to be trimmed when located in the hull and fastened down. Similarly, the deck fittings will be attached to the deck moulding before the deck is fastened to the hull, with the hull-deck join being covered by the toe rail and the headlining or by the joinery. This is much easier than having large numbers of joiners working inside the boat, who have to make numerous journeys between boat and work-bench when fitting the components.

For production on a smaller scale, although the hull and deck will be moulded in the same way, the yard is unlikely to be set up as a production line. There will be more reliance on skilled boatbuilders to fit out the boats, rather than just slot in prefabricated units.

For one-off construction, in most cases foam sandwich is used, laid up over a male mould for the hull, and a male or female mould for the deck. A male mould is used because it ensures that there is less distortion of the cloth when applied and the resin does not drain into the bilge. The hull mould is made from timber frames covered in sheet ply or strip planking. The inside laminate is applied, followed by the core, vacuum-bagged down to ensure a good bond. The work is then faired up, and the final laminate applied, which is subsequently filled and faired to give a smooth finish to the boat. The deck is built in a similar way, but the flatter surfaces mean that a female mould can be used, eliminating the need for the lengthy fairing process. The hull and deck are then broken off the moulds and bonded together. Structural members such as the keel floors and ring frames are bonded in before the interior is fitted.

Wood construction

For one-off construction wood is generally cheaper than plastic, as well as lighter than most plastic sandwich laminates. Although wood has had a bad reputation in terms of long-term maintenance, sheathing the hull below the waterline with a plastic or nylon cloth, and coating the whole hull with epoxy resin has largely overcome the problems. The sheathing keeps out marine borers such as teredo worm, and the epoxy coating keeps the wood dry, thus preserving its strength and preventing rot and staining.

Fig 2.16 *Quarter-tonner being cold moulded over longitudinal stringers, supported by temporary building frames.* (Photo William Payne)

Strip planking is really a modern form of carvel construction. Narrow, almost square-sectioned planks are stretched round the frames and moulds, with each plank being glued and nailed to its neighbour. The glue provides almost all the strength, with the nails increasing the shear strength and acting as crack stoppers. As all the planks run fore-and-aft, the hull is very strong in this direction, but tends to be weak transversely and in torsion. Strength here is largely provided by the transverse frames, but where the frame spacing is large a further contribution can be made by laying up a cold-moulded veneer, or GRP cloth or uni-directional rovings, at an angle of 45 degrees to the planking. GRP cloth is the favourite option, as it makes the boat proof against boring worms and also more resistant to bruising. The problem with strip planking is repairing holes, as the entire damaged area must be cut out to a point beyond any of the glue joins which have cracked, and then new strips must be fitted, scarfed on to the edges of the hole.

Whilst strip planking is most common in the USA, cold moulding is the norm in Europe. Here the hull is generally laminated from three veneers–two diagonally at right angles to each other, and the outermost veneer either perpendicular to the last one or fore and aft. This will be supported by transverse frames, and probably by longitudinal stringers as well (see fig 2.16). Although more labour is required than with a strip-planked boat and the workmanship needs to be of a higher standard, the boat can generally be of lighter construction than with strip planking, as the shell is not biased so much towards longitudinal strength.

Finally, we have hard chine construction in plywood. This has two great advantages: first, it is much quicker than any other method, thus saving greatly on labour costs; and second, it is suitable for amateur construction, as a kit of parts can be produced easily. Against this, the chines can have a serious effect on the appearance of the boat, and a smaller effect on the performance. Many ugly hard-chine boats have been built, generally due to having very slab-sided hulls, but there are also some very attractive designs around, especially those that have some curvature in the panels (though plywood can only bend in one plane at a time). Plywood is also used for decking in most cases, as it is for the interior joinery of almost all boats. Where weight saving is especially important, solid ply can be replaced with panels that have a lightweight foam, honeycomb or balsa core, with a thin ply or veneer on each side.

The rig and sail plan

So far we have only discussed designing the hull for low resistance and stability, and no attention has been paid to the driving force, the sails. The first question to answer is how much sail to carry, in the interests of both the boat's stability and performance. The key ratio here is that of sail area to displacement. A high value indicates plenty of sail, to overcome the frictional resistance (the hull's wetted surface area is proportional to the displacement to the power 1.5) and the wave-making resistance (which is directly proportional to the displacement). However, if this value is too high it is doubtful whether the boat will have sufficient stability to carry the sail in a breeze. As soon as she is reefed the extra length of mast will adversely affect performance, both through the extra windage and the poorer weight distribution.

Fig 2.17 *Sadler 26, a masthead-rigged cruiser. The size of the large genoa can be clearly seen.*
(Photo Sadler Yachts Ltd)

Once the basic sail area has been decided, the next choice is how to distribute it through the rig. In the size of boat we are talking about, there is no advantage whatsoever in going for a second mast, though on a boat designed for short-handed long-distance sailing a cutter rig may be worth considering. A masthead rig is easier to rig and easier to set up satisfactorily. A fractional rig has the advantages of smaller genoas, meaning fewer sails and making sail handling easier, and a mainsail that can easily be powered up or down to suit the conditions. Although the need for runners can be overcome by swept-back spreaders, the resulting flexibility of the rig means that it is more difficult to set up and tune efficiently. In particular, without runners it is very difficult to control mast bend and forestay sag independently, though only the more racing-orientated sailors will bother about this. The fractional rig has a smaller, lower aspect-ratio spinnaker, which can be an advantage in stronger winds and when close reaching, but it does give the masthead rig some superiority on a dead run in most conditions.

Although headsails have generally been designed to a 150 per cent overlap due to the constraints of the IOR and other rating rules, there is a move towards sails with a smaller overlap, in particular towards self-tacking jibs. If the mainsail area is increased to compensate for the smaller jib, or the mast moved aft to increase the jib size, the boat can be tacked single-handed and will still not be short of sail in light airs. If carried to extremes, though, the large mainsail can make the boat very unbalanced in strong winds, especially when reaching without a spinnaker when the boat has most weather helm.

On boats with a self-tacking jib things can also get interesting when the spinnaker is set, as this will be considerably larger in relation to the rest of the rig than would otherwise be the case. Thus, perhaps the best option is to have a fractional-rigged boat, with a fairly large fore triangle to ensure good balance when reefed, and a spinnaker that is probably comparable in size to that of an equivalent masthead rigged boat.

The mast will be supported by a number of sets of spreaders. The more numerous the spreaders, within reason, the lighter and smaller the mast section can be, especially athwartships. However, if the mast section is too flexible it will be difficult to tune the rig so that the mast stays in column and, combined with a smaller factor of safety, it will be more prone to failure.

The position of the chainplates and the width of the spreaders affects how far inboard the larger genoas can be sheeted. The further inboard the chainplates are, the shorter the spreaders can be, and so the further inboard the sail can come – improving windward performance, especially in light airs and flat water. The cost of this, though, is that the compression forces on the mast also increase, and so a larger section is required.

Fore-and-aft support on a masthead rig is provided simply by the forestay and backstay. The lower and intermediate shrouds do have some effect, however, as, if too tight, they will prevent the mast bending enough to flatten out the mainsail in a breeze. On a fractional rig, the support is provided by the forestay and by either runners or swept back shrouds. From a performance point of view runners are preferable, as they give greater control over the mast shape and also allow the main to be squared right off when running. The backstay is used to control bend at the top of the mast, and on a boat without runners it also controls forestay sag. Finally, on a racing boat there will be checkstays attached at a point about half-way between the hounds and the deck, which limit the amount of mast bend low down and so enable the necessary amount of runner tension to be applied, without over-flattening the mainsail.

Keel-stepped masts have the advantage of extra support in the lower region, as the mast is held rigidly at deck level. This enables a slightly lighter section to be used, and due to the extra support the spreaders can be moved higher up the mast. For a cruising boat in particular, though, a deck-stepped mast has the advantage that no water can come into the boat where the mast passes through the deck, and also that the noise of the rigging is not carried into the saloon. For trailer sailers, a deck-stepped mast is essential for ease of stepping and unstepping, and some form of tabernacle arrangement is also highly desirable.

Booms are often ignored at the design stage, with production yacht booms often being just a shorter length of mast section, whilst racing boats tend to have a maxi-depth boom regardless of its advantages. As well as having to be strong enough, the boom also needs to be stiff, or it will bend under load and affect the shape of the lower portion of the mainsail. This is particularly the case when the sail is sheeted from near the middle of the boom. It also needs to be light in weight, as in light airs a heavy boom will pull down on the sail and tighten the leech excessively. The majority of off-the-shelf cruising booms are perfectly strong and stiff enough for the racing yachtsman, and so the only reason in going for a maxi-depth boom is to save weight. In the smaller boats, however, a maxi-depth boom can often work out heavier than an equivalent cruising section, due to the extra size of the boom not being adequately compensated for by the use of a thinner gauge of metal. Another feature often seen on racing yachts is a series of holes in the boom, which can save a little more weight, though not as much as by using a thinner-gauge metal in the first place. These should be covered with adhesive sailcloth to minimize windage, except for the aftermost ones, which should be left open. This allows the mainsail to be freed even when the boom has hit the water, as the holes offer no resistance to it.

Rigging

The standing rigging is almost always made up from 1×19 stainless steel wire, as this has a very long lifespan. Warning that it is reaching the end of its life is often given by stranding at the terminals or the terminals themselves developing cracks. The other alternative is rod rigging which has less stretch and a smaller diameter for a given strength. The low stretch is particularly important with modern racing rigs, as the slender mast section and the narrow chainplate base mean that high rig tension and low stretch are necessary to stop the mast falling off to leeward at the hounds. The disadvantage of rod rigging is the absence of any warning of imminent failure and lower resistance to fatigue. However, improved standards of rigging, together with the practice of stopping each span at the spreader end instead of taking it down to deck level, have gone a long way to solving the problem.

The size of running rigging on a small boat is as often determined by the size that can be easily handled as by strength requirements. In this respect, 10 mm-diameter rope is the minimum if sailing gloves are not worn, though this can be reduced to 6 mm for control lines or light weather sheets if gloves are used. The rope should be braided polyester, as this has low stretch, is soft to handle and grips winch drums well. The use of larger-diameter ropes means that they have to be replaced less frequently, but there is a price to pay as the deck gear often needs to be excessively heavy to take the rope size. The larger-diameter rope also causes a marked increase in friction in the system, making sailing the boat harder work.

For halyards, flexible galvanized wire is preferred, as it has low stretch characteristics and it withstands flexing over the sheaves better than stainless steel wire. The wire has to have a rope tail spliced on. This should be placed so that the splice does not have to be wound round the winch and so that it passes round as few sheaves as possible.

The other material that can be used for halyards and other heavily loaded lines, such as the spinnaker guy and kicking strap, is Kevlar. Although not as resistant to chafe as a wire halyard, for the same strength it is lighter and much easier to handle and is preferred by many foredeck hands for this reason. It is not as resilient as normal polyester rope though, and so needs a larger sheave size. The sheaves should have a flat, rectangular groove rather than a round one, if possible.

Winches and cleats

Winches are essential for the genoa sheets of almost all keelboats, and most will also require winches for halyards and mainsail reef pennants. In the smaller sizes, these will be single-speed winches with a ratchet action. Those with more power will be two speed, so that it is easy to trim the sail once it has been wound in.

There are a number of different materials from which the winch drum can be made. The best of these is generally light alloy as its matt finish results in the rope gripping the winch drum well. However, where a wire halyard goes over the winch drum a more durable material is required, and stainless steel or chromed bronze will be used.

Self-tailing winches make the job of trimming a sail or winding in a halyard much easier when short-handed, and they are equally popular with racing crews as they enable more of the crew to stay on the weather rail.

There needs to be ample room in which to swing the handle, at least 14 in (35 cm) clearance all round. It also needs to be angled so that the rope approaches the winch from slightly the horizontal in order to prevent riding turns.

There are two means of securing the lines led to winches: either each line can have its own winch, with a cleat to take the line where it comes off the drum; or a number of lines can share one winch, each line having its own jammer or stopper forward of the winch. Using the latter method, once the line has been adjusted it is stopped off, and the winch freed for other uses. Although the jammer and stopper will hold the rope equally securely, there is a basic difference in their means of operation. On a jammer the cam securing the rope is operated by the pressure on the rope itself, and to free it when under heavy load it is generally necessary to use the winch to take the strain off the cam. With a stopper, on the other hand, the cam is spring-loaded, and so it can be released no matter what the load. (However, the line will still need to be put round a winch so that it can be released gradually once the stopper is let off.)

3

FITTING THE BOAT TO THE CREW

In the last chapter we concentrated on hull and rig design in the abstract, with little regard to the crew's requirements. In this chapter we shall redress the balance, looking at how the crew fit into the boat.

One fact that must always be borne in mind is that a given hull design has only a finite amount of space, and so the amount of accommodation is also finite. Thus, the designer must reach a satisfactory compromise between all the accommodation requirements, and the more he wants to include, the less space each item can occupy. To some extent he can make matters easier for himself by drawing up a hull with a very large interior volume – full ended and with wide slab-sided sections, together with high freeboard and heavy displacement – but if pushed too far this may damage the sailing properties of the boat excessively.

Designing the cockpit

A large cockpit is essential for racing boats, to give the crew plenty of room to work in. On a cruising boat, especially one intended for use in warmer climes, a large cockpit is also desirable. However, the size of cockpit and its design must be balanced against the requirements of the layout below decks.

From a safety point of view, the cockpit must not be too large, as if the boat were pooped or hit by a large wave the cockpit could easily hold a ton of water or more, lowering the stern and making the boat more likely to be swamped by another wave. Furthermore, the boat must have good-sized cockpit drains or an open transom, and it must be possible to seal off the cockpit from the interior by making the hatches and, where appropriate, the locker lids watertight. In the main

Fig 3.1 A Jenneau Sun Fast half-tonner. Note the large cockpit for easy crew work, and the coachroof which is the minimum size required by the rules. The fine bow and flared, beamy after sections of the IOR boat are clearly visible.
(Photo Tony Castro)

companionway hatch, where the opening extends below deck level, it must be possible to close off the vertical part with washboards and secure them in place so that they do not drop out in the event of a knockdown. In heavy weather a perspex washboard helps reassure those down below that the helmsman is still on board, and in more moderate conditions it also allows a large amount of light to get down below.

Although a large cockpit is a great boon in warm climates, if it is much over 6 ft (1.8 m) in length it means that space is lost down below aft of the quarter berths. This space can be utilised by having a cockpit locker right aft, but as this will almost certainly be below the tiller, access when actually sailing will be a problem.

Cockpit lockers are a great asset on cruising boats, allowing sails, warps and fenders to be stowed outside the living space. They must be sensibly designed, though, so that there is good access and proper stowage for individual items, rather than a case of simply throwing everything into the cavern and then having to rummage around to find anything.

So far we have not considered the depth of the cockpit. A shallow cockpit leaves more height over the quarter berths, and also makes it easier for a racing crew to work the boat. However, cruising yachtsmen prefer a deeper cockpit, generally with cockpit seats inboard of a coaming, to give a greater degree of security and protection from the elements. If the cockpit is too deep, though, it becomes a major operation to climb in and out of it, and the height of the coamings and coachroof above the cockpit seats also reduces the arc of visibility.

Siting the helmsman

The helmsman must have a good view forwards, both to look at the sails and waves and to see possible hazards. He (or she) needs to be able to see the instruments, especially the compass, but also the log, wind instruments and echo sounder Furthermore, he must have a good, secure seating arrangement. Downwind, he may sit in the cockpit, but upwind, in anything of a breeze he will need to sit up on the sidedeck or cockpit coaming, so that he has a good field of vision. In both positions he must be able to brace himself securely, either against the leeward side of the cockpit or against footrests. Furthermore, no winches or other deck fittings should be sited so that the helmsman has to move for the crew to operate them.

Coachroof design

The coachroof, like the cockpit, is another major meeting point of interior and exterior design. The wider the coachroof and the further forward it extends, the greater the area down below with good headroom, but the more cluttered the deck becomes – unless the coachroof is carried right outboard to the gunwale, as was once fashionable, which gives the best of both worlds. Failing this, a coachroof should not leave less than a foot (30 cm) of sidedeck each side for the crew to be able to walk safely, and twice this amount is really required to sunbathe on.

Although a high coachroof is regarded as ugly, particularly if it is narrow or if the boat has low freeboard, it is often essential to give the full standing headroom required on many production yachts. Furthermore, in severe weather conditions it contributes to improving the large angle stability of the boat. The height can be disguised in a number of ways by careful

Fig 3.2 *E-boat. The flush deck is ideal for sunbathing and racing, but it severely reduces the headroom below decks.* (Photo Sadler Yachts Ltd)

styling. Examples of this are using a large amount of camber in both the deck and coachroof, and breaking it up visually with a broad contrasting stripe along its length.

Layout down below

In the case of the relatively small boats which we are talking about, the designer is virtually forced to adopt an open-plan

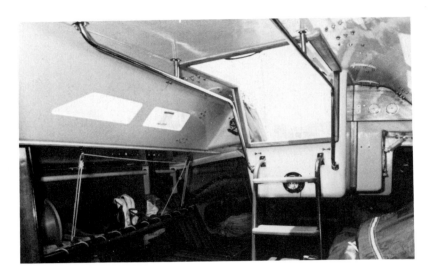

layout. If he tries to emulate bigger boats with full-height
bulkheads dividing the boat up into separate cabins, the
interior will seem claustrophobic, and the very existence of the
bulkheads and doors will use up an appreciable amount of the
available space.

Racing interiors

There are a number of alternatives for the layout down below.
The simplest of these is on the racing yacht where there are
pipe cots from mast to stern on each side, enabling the entire
off-watch crew to stay to weather. Pipe cots are used because,
although not pretty, they can be hoisted up to the angle of heel
of the boat, which means that they are the most comfortable
type of berth at sea. As far as the rest of the accommodation is
concerned, there will be a lightweight chemical toilet, often
empty to save weight, and a minimal galley with stowage for
sandwiches, chocolate bars, canned foods, instant coffee, etc.
The chart table will also be rather rudimentary, as virtually all
of the navigation during the race will be done from the weather
rail, so that weight is kept in the optimum position at all times.

Forepeak

Although the racing boat is very well suited to its intended
purpose, most of us would really prefer something a little more

comfortable. On a cruising yacht there will almost always be a twin V-berth or a double berth in the bows, though it is often only large enough for children. The boat's motion is most severe up forward, and so these berths will often be unusable at sea, except as an extension to the stowage area. On a boat designed for serious cruising, rather than weekend sailing, these berths may well be sacrificed, and the forward area occupied by sail stowage space, a small workbench, and perhaps the heads as well.

Saloon

Moving amidships to the main saloon area, the norm here is for a settee berth on each side of the boat, with stowage or an extra pilot berth outboard if the size of the boat permits. On smaller boats, though, the galley and chart table may be

Fig 3.4 *Interior of a Jaguar 25, showing the dinette arrangement.* (Photo Jaguar Yachts)

Fig 3.5 *Harrier 20, a simple*
weekend cruiser, with two berths
each side, heads in the bow, and a
small galley under the
companionway. (Jo Aldridge)

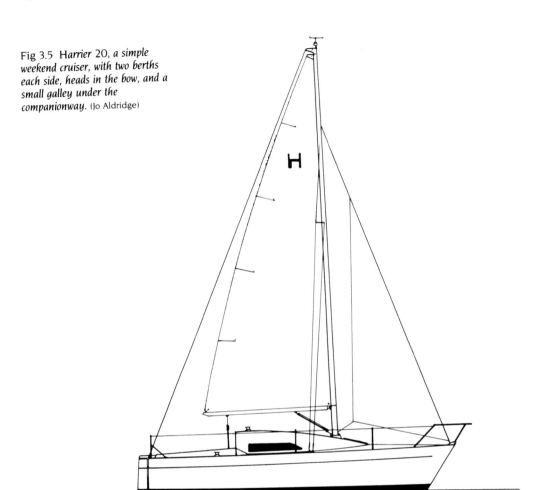

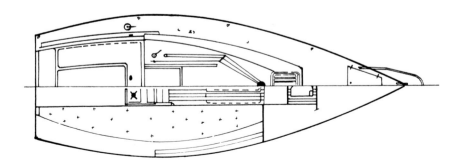

placed along one side of the saloon, giving more space aft for quarter berths or a heads compartment. Alternatively, there may be a dinette on one side, with a saloon table and seats running athwartships (see fig 3.4). Although this works out very well in harbour, particularly if the table can be dropped to form a double berth, at sea one will always be sliding down to the leeward end of the seats when the boat is heeled. Furthermore, in order to keep the dinette arrangement far enough to the side of the saloon, the cabin sole often has to be raised, and this reduces headroom somewhat.

Going back to the conventional case of saloon berths running fore-and-aft, often there is not quite enough length for a full-size berth. If the berth butts onto a locker at the foot end, a footwell about 12 in (30 cm) high can project forwards into the locker space. This must be carefully designed if it is to be comfortable when the boat is heeled, so that there is no thin web of material that will cut into the occupant's legs when he or she is lying against the side of the berth. This warning applies not only to footwells, as tie rods for the chainplates, or occasionally transverse frames, can also be culprits.

Whatever the arrangement of the berths, they should still cater for the same size of occupant, and so there is no excuse whatsoever for reducing the berth size. Each berth needs to be 6 ft 6 in (2 m) long and 26–30 in (66–76 cm) wide at the head, tapering towards the foot. A double berth needs to be 4 ft (1.2 m) wide at the head, and there should also be the facility to erect a divide down the middle, so that two people can use it in comfort at sea.

Galley layout

The galley requirements will depend greatly on the sort of sailing planned. If this will largely be confined to racing or day sailing, little more is required than a small cooker to boil a kettle or heat up a stew, a sink, and stowage for sandwiches and a thermos flask. In fact, not even this is essential: soups and stews can be heated up beforehand and kept hot in wide-mouthed thermos flasks. However, most people will want more space than this, with more worktop space, more stowage lockers, and perhaps an ice box too.

Traditionally, the galley is placed on the port side of the boat. The justification for this is that, if the boat is sailing along on port tack and suddenly has to go about in order to give way to another vessel, the contents of the galley will merely slide against the side of the boat instead of falling onto the cabin sole. This argument is not a very strong one, though, as it seems to imply that a proper watch is not being maintained. A more important criterion, in my view, concerns where the cook stands in relation to the galley. With the majority of people being right-handed, the cook should be to the left of the galley, so that most items can be reached by the right hand. A similar consideration applies to the chart table. All too often the navigator is forced to sit at the right-hand end of the chart table, with his or her writing arm cramped up against a bulkhead.

The cooker is clearly central to any galley. On a small boat there may not be room for anything more than a two-burner unit, but an oven is well worth fitting whenever space permits (in my opinion it is of even more use than a grill). An entire meal can be prepared ashore in disposable aluminium containers and then simply heated up in the oven. Moreover, food can easily be kept warm in the oven until after a sail change or until the other half of the crew come off watch. The other indispensable item is a pressure cooker. If of adequate size, it can cook an entire meal for the crew, and it is ideal for use at sea both because of the short cooking times and, perhaps most importantly, because the pressure-tight lid means that the contents cannot be spilled, no matter how rough the conditions.

For sailing in warm climates, an ice box is a great asset, so long as ice is readily obtainable. The box does result in quite a lot of space being lost, though, as it really needs 4 inches (100 mm) of insulation all round it to work efficiently. As a result, it may be best not to have it in the galley, and alternative positions may be in the forepeak or inside a cockpit locker. The box should have a volume of at least 2.5 cu. ft (70 l) if it is to prove worthwhile, but if too large it becomes inefficient when half full, and two smaller ice boxes would be better. The actual box should be of plastic or plastic-covered laminate, with a drain to take away the melted ice and a lid with a flange

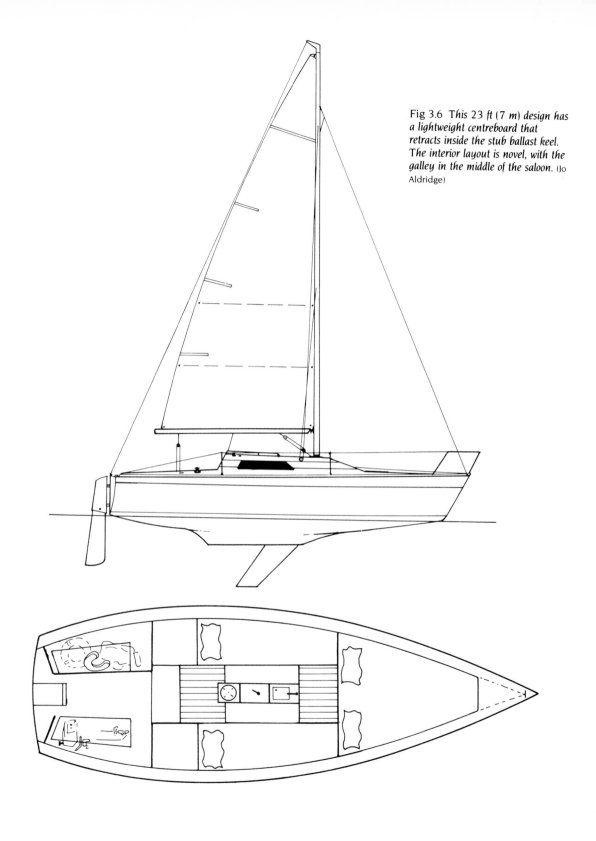

Fig 3.6 This 23 ft (7 m) design has a lightweight centreboard that retracts inside the stub ballast keel. The interior layout is novel, with the galley in the middle of the saloon. (Jo Aldridge)

to help keep the temperature low. The ice should go in first, with the food and drink on top, and it should ideally be kept completely full. A large solid lump of ice will last longer than loose cubes, though it will not cool the contents of the box as quickly, because the air can only reach a much smaller surface of the cold ice.

The commonest layout is an L-shaped galley right by the companionway. This works well, as everything is close to hand and it does not take up an excessive amount of the accommodation space. Furthermore, being close to the companionway ensures good ventilation and makes it easy for the crew members to slip down below and put the kettle on. If space is limited, the galley can be split between the two sides of the boat, with the stove on one side and the sink on the other. If the boat is too wide this becomes awkward, as one is always stretching out from one side of the boat to the other. Moreover, if people are continually passing between the cockpit and the saloon, it will quickly wear on the cook's nerves. What does not work at all, however, is siting the galley at the base of the companionway steps. Sooner or later one of the crew will add an unwanted pinch of sailing boot to the cook's creation. In addition, it is often too draughty there for the cooker to stay alight with the flame turned down low.

An arrangement that works well on very small cruisers is to run the galley down one side of the saloon, which means that the cook can do all the cooking sitting on the saloon seat. Although this is a good arrangement for cooking at sea, the crew and guests lose out in not being able to sit round a table, a much more sociable arrangement than having everyone strung out along one side of the boat.

The galley needs a large number of small lockers, rather than a few enormous ones, so that all the bits and pieces necessary for preparing a meal are close to hand. There is no need to store all the food in the galley, and it is generally better to keep just the everyday items and the food required for the next few meals there, with the rest being stored elsewhere. All the lockers should ideally be accessible even when a meal is in the middle of preparation. Only too often one finds that one cannot get to the lockers behind the stove without risk of burning oneself, or that in order to get at a locker lid let into the

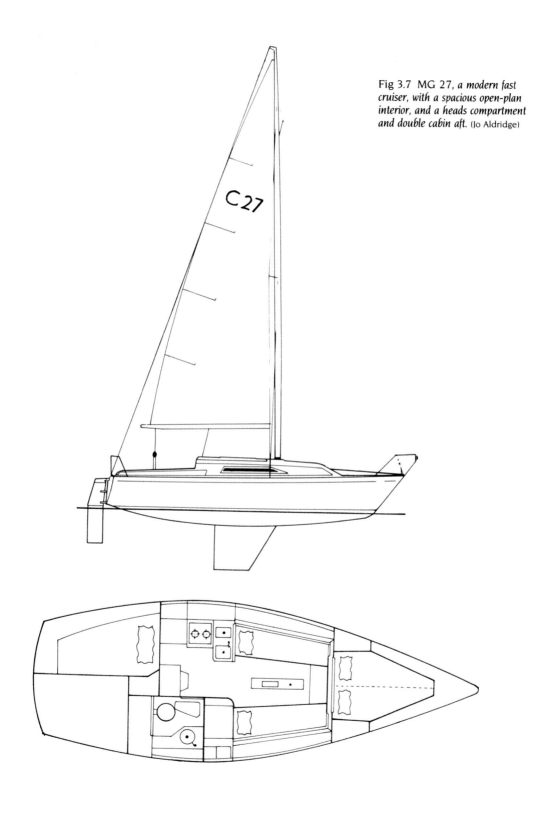

Fig 3.7 MG 27, *a modern fast cruiser, with a spacious open-plan interior, and a heads compartment and double cabin aft.* (Jo Aldridge)

worktop one has to put all the prepared food onto the chart table or saloon table.

As it is often necessary to have several items out on the worktop when cooking at sea, there must be good high fiddles, preferably dividing up the worktop space if it is large. Also, to stop the cook being thrown around, a galley strap will be required for him or her to lean against. If most of the cooking is done at anchor, much of this is not required and the deep fiddles necessary at sea just get in the way. To circumvent this problem some boats have fiddles that can be folded down when not required.

Heads arrangement

The smallest keelboats have the heads in the bows between the halves of the V-berth, or possibly under one of the seats. One successful idea here is to site the heads under the navigator's seat, as this is often in a corner of the boat and so a curtain can easily be drawn round the area to give some privacy.

In bigger boats a separate heads compartment can be built in. This can either be forward, between the saloon and the forepeak, or at the aft end of the cabin to one side of the companionway. Although having it aft means that a quarter berth is lost, the space aft of the heads can be used to make a spacious deck locker. In this position there is generally more headroom, more space and an easier motion than forward, though it can also impinge on the space required by the galley or the chart table. If the heads are forward, the full height bulkhead completely separates the forecabin from the rest of the boat. This gives privacy to the occupants, but tends to make the interior look smaller and often makes it a bit of a struggle to get from the forepeak to the saloon, especially carrying sails or other bulky items.

The finish in the heads department is particularly important, especially if a shower is installed, as it will probably be the wettest part of the interior. The ideal solution is really to have a one-piece plastic moulding for the entire compartment, with a moulded-in sump to collect water from the shower and from oilskins hung up to dry. Good ventilation is also important, so that moist air can be expelled and the build-up of condensation minimised, and also so that odours can be dispersed.

Chart table

In many small boats a chart table is dispensed with, and the saloon table used for chartwork instead. This is perfectly acceptable for the many boats that undertake only relatively short passages, normally in the same sailing area, especially if there is proper stowage for charts, books and instruments close to hand. As boats go further afield, though, the need for a chart table increases.   The table really needs to be at least 20 in (50 cm) square, otherwise it is not worth having at all, and an area of 24 × 30 in (61 × 76 cm) is a much better target to aim for. In most boats it does not need to be a permanent fixture: it can just as easily fold or slide out of the way when not in use, or double as an extra worktop for the galley. Furthermore, there is no real need to be able to sit at the chart table. In fact, when well heeled it is often more comfortable and more practical to stand when navigating, especially if the layout makes one sit facing outboard. The positioning of the chart table is standard in almost all boats – at the aft end of the settee berth, or the forward end of a quarter berth. It is nice if

Fig 3.8 *Westerly Merlin, showing the aft cabin and heads.*
(Photo Westerly Yachts Ltd)

the berth is long, so that it can still be occupied while the navigator is working.

Ventilation

Every boat needs good ventilation, both to give a good circulation of air when nobody is on board, thus minimising the build-up of condensation and the risk of mould, and to prevent the air growing stale when people are living on board. It is essential when cooking, as apart from producing cooking smells the cooker will rapidly use up the oxygen down below.

The ventilation must be such that there can still be good air circulation in the roughest of conditions. Reliance on the foredeck and companionway hatches is not enough, as they will let water in as soon as spray starts coming over the deck. Instead, ports opening into the cockpit can be used, together with one of the various forms of vent available, some of which incorporate a small solar-powered fan, so that a flow of air is maintained even when the boat is unmanned. A low profile vent is less likely to catch ropes, but the height of a cowl vent, together with the ability to swivel it around to point in any direction, means that it is much less likely to let water come down below. Whichever sort of vent is fitted, there should be a means of shutting it off – preferably from down below – so that the interior can be sealed off in bad weather.

Water supply

Each member of the yacht's crew will use about a gallon (4.5 l) of water every day if left to his or her own devices, though this amount can be halved without excessive discomfort. Each gallon of water weighs 10 1b (4.5 kg), and occupies a cube with sides of about 6½ inches (17 cm). This may not seem much, but for a crew of four it means that for a month's cruise about half a ton (500 kg) of water will be carried, occupying a cube with edges of about 32 in (80 cm). On a small boat this represents quite a lot of weight and stowage space. That is why so many production boats have a tank capacity more suited to weekend sailing, sacrificing adequate volume to provide a more spacious interior.

The tanks need to be kept as low down and as central in the boat as possible, as their heavy weight when full can have a significant effect on the boat's stability and trim. The water is best divided between two or more tanks, with a shut-off valve to each tank. Then if one tank springs a leak there will still be fresh water on board, and also when the boat is used for short journeys only one tank need be kept topped up. The tanks are probably best made from light alloy, as plastic tanks often taint the water and flexible tanks, though cheap and simple to fit, can burst in severe weather if not installed correctly.

In addition to cold fresh water, the ready availability of hot water on a cruising boat makes life much more pleasant. As the heat output of a small boat's engine is fairly low and the engine is unlikely to be run that often, fitting a calorifier to heat the water by the engine coolant is not really effective. Instead, a through-flow gas heater provides the best solution, so long as it is properly installed. Like any other open flame, it will consume oxygen from the air and emit a considerable amount of waste heat. Thus, installing the unit in an unventilated heads compartment is not a good idea, as the shortage of fresh air will result in the flame emitting poisonous carbon monoxide instead of carbon dioxide as the oxygen level drops. A better solution is to mount the unit in the saloon, where there is a plentiful supply of fresh air, and the waste heat from the unit will also help keep the saloon warm. A flue will also be required, suitably insulated where it passes through the deck, if a shower is fitted, or any other appliance that will use more than a few minutes' worth of hot water at a time. For safety's sake it is probably best to install the flue in any case.

Keeping the engine quiet

One of the attractions of sailing is that it is an essentially quiet means of getting from A to B. It is always an intrusion when calms or schedules require the engine to be started up. Good design, though, can go a long way to minimising the sound levels emitted by the engine.

Noise comes not only directly from the engine and gearbox, but also from vibration of the hull by the engine and pressure waves of the propeller. To control this noise a number of steps can be taken. First of all, having the engine flexibly mounted largely isolates its vibration from the rest of the boat's structure, thereby reducing the noise transmitted to the interior. Second, the clearance between the propeller and the hull can be increased, reducing the amount of noise created by the propeller. If possible the interior can be designed so that there are no accommodation areas immediately above the propeller, where noise is greatest. Third, the engine box should be very rigid (eg thick plywood) and have a sound absorbing layer on the inside, such as the lead/foam or mineral wool sheets that are available. The apertures to the engine space should be as few and as small as possible, provided there is sufficient access for the engine's air supply. Finally, low-revving engines and propellers are generally quieter than high-revving ones, and the lower frequency of their noise spectrum makes the noise less penetrating.

Stowage

It is all too easy to overlook stowage requirements when looking at a design. Stowage can be split into three basic categories: boat equipment, clothes and personal effects, and food.

The bulkiest items of boat gear to store are without doubt the sails. On a cruising boat, where the sails are of a soft cloth, they can easily be folded into a fairly small sailbag which can go into a cockpit locker or into the forepeak. The sail materials more likely to be found on racing yachts – Kevlar, Mylar and heavily resinated Dacron – must be folded as little as possible, and so the sails are generally stowed in long bags, whose length is about half the foot length of the sail, and kept on the cabin sole or under the cockpit. There should also be the capacity for stowing headsails on the foredeck, as often the wind strength keeps alternating between the ranges of two sails. A length of shockcord running along each side of the foredeck, with a plastic snap hook in the middle, can easily be clipped over the sail and onto the guardrail or toerail once the sail has been dropped and will keep it in place so long as solid water is not coming across the deck. There should also be a lacing of light line from the toerail up to the top guardrail on

Fig 3.9 *Anchor stowage and stem fitting. Ideally, a lashing or pin would secure the anchor, and a bronze roller would stand up to the chain longer than the nylon one fitted here.*

either side from the pulpit aft to level with the mast, and up to the lower guardrail some distance aft of this, to stop sails going over the side when dropped.

The other major items of gear are warps, fenders and anchoring equipment. On a cruising boat these are best kept in a deck locker for ease of access, with at least one anchor stowed either in a locker in the bows or on the stem fitting (see fig 3.9). On a racing yacht, though, all these weights will be centralised to improve the weight distribution as much as possible, and they will be stowed in the saloon as low down as possible. Furthermore, in order to minimise the weight of the boat, only the minimum amount of gear required by the rules will be carried.

In a small boat there is not a great deal of room for lockers, and most of the stowage for clothes and personal effects is to be found underneath the bunks and settees. The major problem when stowing personal gear is to keep it dry, and keep bilge water out of the lockers. Ideally, each locker should have all its sides bonded to the hull at the bottom, so that water cannot penetrate from one locker to another; at the very least, the area under the saloon floorboards must be isolated from the rest of the bilges, so that bilge water cannot get into the locker spaces. Failing this, the lockers can be fitted with PVC liners, or the crew can keep their gear in waterproof kit bags (this is worth doing in any case, as it encourages everyone to keep their gear together in one place). On longer voyages the chances of water getting into stowage spaces is even greater, and so items not regularly required should be stowed inside stout waterproof bags. In addition, items that need to be kept dry should be divided between a number of lockers, so if the worst comes to the worst at least some of the clothes are likely to remain dry.

Wet weather gear should also have its own storage area, though this is not always possible in smaller boats. To have any chance of drying out, oilskins need to be hung up in a well ventilated space, so the water can drain off. When hung up, they should ideally be turned inside out first, so that the condensation that inevitably forms inside oilskins has a chance to dry out before the next watch. If there is not a special oilskin locker, the heads compartment is probably the best stowage area as it is designed to contain the water that will drip off.

Storing tinned food is not a problem, unless it is stowed where it is likely to get wet, when the contents should be written on the tin with a waterproof pen and the label removed so that it does not clog up the bilge pumps. On true long-distance voyages it can be worth coating the tins with varnish or similar to try and prevent rusting, because eventually the metal will corrode through and the contents be spoiled. Fresh or dried food needs to be kept dry, preferably in a cool, dark, well-ventilated locker, for maximum life, although good-quality food will keep a surprisingly long time with the minimum of special treatment. Paper bags or cardboard boxes are obviously not a good idea for a boat, and the contents should be transferred to plastic containers.

Fire precautions

Fire is a major hazard at sea, and steps should be taken to minimise the likelihood of an outbreak, or if the worst happens

Fig 3.10 *Bow well. The strap is for the gas bottle, perhaps a bit vulnerable if stowed with the anchor. Note how the pulpit has been shaped to hold a spinnaker turtle.*

to minimise its spread. Unfortunately, there are no legal requirements for fireproof materials to be fitted, though racing yachts are required to carry a pair of fire extinguishers.

To begin with the hull structure, standard GRP hulls are flammable. However, fire-retardant resins are available at the cost of slightly inferior structural properties, and when they are used in conjunction with heavy woven rovings for the outer layer of the laminate the spread of fire can be contained. A further improvement is in the use of fire-retardant fabrics for the cushion covers and curtains, and also for the actual cushions. Suitable materials are not only difficult to set alight, but also they do not emit toxic fumes when heated or alight .

The next area demanding attention is the installation of the engine, fuel tank and cooker. The fuel tank needs to be robustly constructed and well secured. The fuel lines themselves should be copper pipe with short flexible sections to isolate them from the vibration of the engine. Underneath the engine there should be a drip tray, to catch drips of fuel or oil from the engine and prevent their slopping around in the bilges. There should be an electrical connection between the fuel filler plate on deck and the tank, to prevent the build-up of static electricity when filling the tank, which can cause sparks. The filler pipe should extend almost to the bottom of the tank so that a liquid seal is formed in the pipe, limiting the spread of flames into the tank.

Gas installations like the cooker and, perhaps, a heater for water or for the cabin are often a source of worry, as a gas leak is potentially catastrophic. Perhaps the safest installation is where the gas bottle screws directly onto the underside of the cooker, as there is no vulnerable piping at all. Unfortunately, this takes up a considerable amount of space and also removes the possibility of having an oven. The other safe type of installation has the gas bottle kept in a deck locker, sealed off from the rest of the boat, with a vent in the bottom for water and leaking gas to drain outside the boat. The piping is then led to the various appliances inside the boat, as high up the boat's side as possible so that any escaping gas can disperse through the boat, and not accumulate in the bilges.

If there is a fire, the crew need to have a means of getting up on deck. To ensure that this is possible there should be a fore hatch as well as the main companionway hatch, so that wherever the fire breaks out the crew do not have to struggle through the flames to find an escape route.

4

NAVIGATION

In the size of boat that we are dealing with, navigation facilities tend to be rather restricted. On racing boats we have already discussed how performance suffers if the crew have to come in from the windward rail, and so the skipper may be loath to let the navigator spend hours poring over the charts down below. In addition, due to the IOR's restriction on crew numbers the navigator will generally be needed on deck for sail changes, mark roundings and other operations.

On cruising boats, especially production boats, there is always the temptation to have a larger saloon or galley in preference to a decent-sized chart table, since the illusion of extra space helps to sell the boat. As a result, the navigator has to use a foldaway chart table or share the saloon table, and he or she often has to occupy a sea berth when working at the chart table.

As in all design matters, a compromise has to be reached, and the buyer must decide whether or not the arrangement meets his (or her) needs. If he intends to sail extensively inshore with a small crew, then a separate chart table is well worth having, as he can afford the space and will be referring to the charts often. On the other hand, if there is a large crew the accommodation requirements may severely restrict the options when it comes to the navigation area, and he may well decide that a table that slides out of the way under the cockpit sole or folds up against a bulkhead or the side of the hull, is preferable. If much of his sailing is truly offshore, he will often only be taking a fix once or twice a day, and for this type of sailing it may well be preferable to use the saloon table for navigation so the space saved can be used for stowage.

Instruments

The smaller the boat, the simpler the instrumentation it usually carries. This is not because a small boat necessarily needs less instrumentation (though it is easier to sail 'by the seat of the pants' than a large boat), but because the cost of instruments is fixed and so represents a greater proportion of the boat's total cost.

Compass

This is the most basic of all instruments, and a steering compass mounted within sight of the helmsman is essential for even the smallest of boats that venture out into open waters. One never knows when fog may close in, and even the most experienced of sailors become disorientated in these conditions.

It is worth looking at the various options for siting the compass in some detail, as most of the principles apply equally well to any other instruments with their displays visible on deck. The two options are either a deck-mounted type let into the deck just forward of the helmsman, or a through-bulkhead mounting sited on the bulkhead at the forward end of the cockpit.

If deck-mounted, one compass is needed on each side of the boat, positioned forward of the helmsman where he (or she) can see it from all normal steering positions, and where it is not likely to be obscured or sat upon by another crew member. The chief advantages are, due to its being mounted so close to the helmsman, it is easy to read and there is less chance of crew members obscuring it. However, when steering solely by the compass the helmsman is constantly switching his attention from looking up at the sails and waves to looking down at the compass card.

If mounted on the bulkhead, the compass falls neatly within the helm's arc of vision, especially if there is one on each side of the boat rather than just a single compass on the centreline. It can also be seen more readily by the navigator and other crew members, which is especially useful if one of the crew is delegated to call the windshifts when beating or running. Depending upon the model of compass fitted, it may be possible to read it from both the front and the back, in which case it can also be read by the navigator from the chart table. However, as the compass is further away from the helm it must be easy to read. This is particularly important on a long passage at night, when the combination of the dark and fatigue can make concentrating on the instruments extremely difficult.

Log and boat speed

Next to the compass, this is perhaps the most essential instrument. The transducer is normally either a paddle wheel or an impeller, mounted on the centreline approximately midway between the forefoot and the leading edge of the keel. The display is either in the cockpit or by the chart table. The display may be either analogue (a dial with a needle) or digital. Personal preference largely determines the cruising yachtsman's choice here, but for racing boats a digital display is virtually essential to give the resolution and speed of response necessary when continuously trimming the sails and altering course for maximum speed.

Cruising boat owners may well prefer to have at least the distance run displayed by the chart table, where it can be seen by the navigator. However, racing boats will need to have the boat speed displayed in the cockpit, preferably where it can

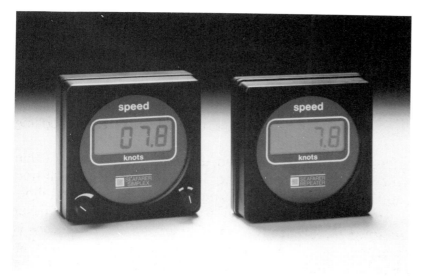

Fig 4.1 *Log main display and on-deck repeater.* (Photo Seafarer Navigation International Ltd)

be seen by both the helmsman and the sail-trimmers. Many cruising sailors,too, like to have a boat speed repeater in the cockpit (see fig 4.1).

One aspect of using a log that is not given all the attention it deserves is calibration. As the water flows past underneath the hull it is accelerated as it approaches amidships and then retarded as it carries on to the stern. The instrument manufacturer cannot predict the exact magnitude of this error, as it depends upon hull form, displacement and boat size, as well as the exact location of the transducer. Thus he sets the log to a reasonable value for most boats, but this may still be 10 per cent out on your boat. Obviously, an error of this magnitude can put your dead reckoning out by quite a distance. Errors in the log become even more significant if it is integrated with the wind instruments and compass to provide data such as true wind speed and direction.

Calibrate the log over a measured distance, preferably on a day when the wind and sea are calm. First of all, check that the log reads the same on both tacks. If the log readings are different, with the same sail settings, the impeller is probably not properly aligned parallel to the centreline, and it should be rotated until the same readings are obtained on both tacks. Now, with the throttle at a fixed setting, motor the distance in one direction, and then motor back again, timing each run with a stopwatch. If the average speed for the two runs combined is not the same as the log reading, the calibration should be changed, or if this is not possible the correction factor should be kept in the chart table. Note that if the impeller is removed it will need to be recalibrated, and so this should be one of the regular features of the annual refit.

Echo sounder

A good echo sounder is an essential item of equipment. The echo sounder, and how quickly the reading changes, enables the racing man to decide when to tack into deeper water or when he is moving into or out of the stronger tidal stream associated with a deeper channel of water. It enables the cruising man to keep a sensible distance offshore, and when he wants to anchor it tells him the depth of water. If used in conjunction with tidal calculations, the depth can also be used

Fig 4.2 *Echo sounder, incorporating both a rotating light and a digital display, together with a depth alarm.*
(Photo Seafarer Navigation International Ltd)

to cross-check the navigation. However, the signal is dependent upon the nature of the sea bed, with a softer bottom giving a weaker signal, and in soft mud some of the less powerful models may not return a signal at all.

The echo sounder may either be of the rotating type, where a light flashes against the scale once per revolution, or the newer type giving a digital read out. An example of a combination of both types is shown in figure 4.2. A graph display is also available, where a trace of the depth is plotted on a screen or on paper, thus indicating how quickly the depth is changing. Whichever type is fitted, it is important to be able to read it from the helm, as otherwise one crew member will have to be down below all the time when sailing in shallow water, watching the echo sounder readings.

Wind instruments

There is a large variation in the degree of complexity of wind instruments, varying from a simple burgee or wind indicator at the masthead to a sophisticated set of computerised instruments that interface with an electronic compass and the boat's log.

In most cases, a vane-type wind indicator is perfectly

Fig 4.3 *Mariner Micro-10*
instrument display, giving wind
speed and direction, velocity made
good (VMG) and sailing efficiency.
(Photo Mariner Electronics)

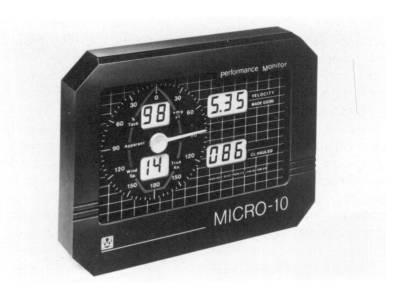

adequate for cruising or for racing helmsmen who prefer to sail
'by the seat of their pants'. It is much preferable to a burgee,
which is not sensitive enough to provide an accurate indication
of the wind direction. Some models of masthead light
incorporate a mount for the wind indicator and a small light in
the top that illuminates it at night.

One step up from this is a deck-level display of apparent
wind speed and angle. The display of wind angle saves the
helmsman having to look up at the masthead, and is of
particular use when close hauled or running so long as it is a
digital or magnified analogue display, when it can register very
small changes in wind angle, and so help the helmsman keep
the boat 'in the groove' upwind and at the best angle
downwind. The wind speed display is a useful indication of
which sails should be set, though the exact change-over point
is determined as much by the sea state as by the wind speed,
especially on lighter boats. With a bit of plotting by the
navigator, the wind data can also be used to predict the
apparent wind speed on the next leg of the course.

Finally, there are sailing instruments that integrate the wind
data, boat speed and often an electronic compass (see fig 4.3).

The more sophisticated versions may also be interfaced with echo sounder, autopilot, Decca, Loran or Satnav. Until recently, the price of instrumentation to these standards was prohibitively expensive, but this has now fallen to a level where it can be justified for a committed racing yachtsman, and no doubt in time the cost will fall further.

In their most basic form, three powerful new possibilities are opened up. First, the combination of compass and log can give you a dead-reckoning position, normally measured as a course and distance from a given starting point, and from this you can get your average speed. Obviously, this still needs to be corrected for tide and leeway, but it is a great improvement on the helmsman having to estimate the course and speed which he has averaged over his last watch.

Second, combining wind data, boat speed and compass direction gives true wind speed and direction, which means that one can immediately tell what sails are needed on the next leg without having to plot out boat speed and apparent wind vectors.

Finally, VMG (Velocity Made Good) is available. This is the component of the boat's speed directly into the wind, and so getting a large positive number indicates a good combination of course and boat speed to windward, whilst a large negative number indicates the same downwind. However, VMG must be used with some caution, and one cannot sail to it as one would to a compass. For example, on the beat if the helmsman heads up a bit more VMG will always increase at first, just due to the time it takes for the boat to slow down. When VMG starts to decline the helmsman may decide to bear off, but now VMG will continue to drop initially until the boat accelerates. Thus, if sailing by the VMG display alone, there is a tendency to shoot the boat up into the wind until she has lost her way, then bear off to build up speed, and so never actually settle onto the best course. A similar phenomenon will be seen off the wind, but not nearly so pronounced, as the boat's speed changes less with changes in course. In my experience, it is best to use VMG as a guide to whether or not you are doing well, and then use the apparent wind angle and the boatspeed indicators to decide whether you want to head up or bear away from your present course.

The main problem with these integrated systems is that, although the sensors may be accurate, the program that analyses the data may not be up to the job. Unfortunately, one can only tell whether or not this is so by using the instruments on the water. Signs of poor instrumentation are that the true wind direction alters between tacks or that the true wind speed varies between when the boat is beating and when she is running. Also, it may not be possible to set the damping so that a satisfactory compromise is reached between having the displayed data jumping all over the place whenever the boat hits a wave and having the instrument so heavily damped, to give a steady display, that it takes an excessively long time for changes in the course steered or the wind direction to be registered.

Radio direction finding
This is still the main form of position fixing for small yachts, because it offers good coverage in all popular sailing areas, extending far enough out to sea to cover most coastal and inshore voyages, and the receiving equipment is both inexpensive and reliable. At best it is accurate to two degrees – in other words a cross-track error of 1.7 miles at a range of 50 miles, but often a weak signal, or deflection of the signal by the land, will increase the errors considerably.

The RDF set basically consists of a radio receiver that can receive transmissions from navigational radio beacons, a unidirectional aerial and a compass to read off the bearing of the beacon. This can be in a self-contained hand-held unit used solely for RDF work (fig 4.4), or the RDF aerial and compass can be in a separate hand-held unit which plugs into the boat's radio receiver. My preference is for the latter arrangement, as in most cases one will use the RDF set at the chart table, and the boat's main radio receiver will generally give better reception than an all-in-one RDF set. The main exception to this is with metal hulls, as the hull effectively prevents any radio signals from being picked up inside the vessel and so one has to operate the set with the aerial on deck.

The main problem with most RDF installations is that of electrical interference. This is most likely to arise from the

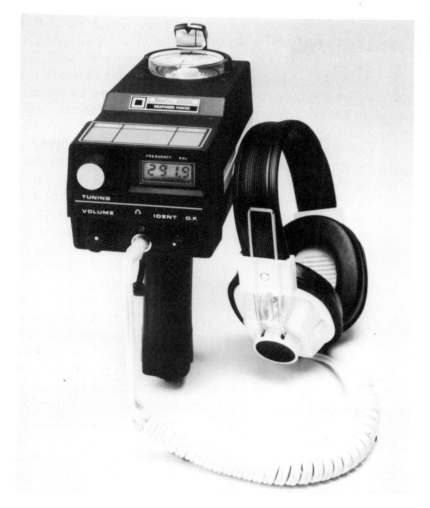

Fig 4.4 *Self-contained radio direction finder.* (Photo Seafarer Navigation International Ltd)

engine's electrics when under power, from the instruments (especially the echo sounder), from fluorescent lights and from the autopilot. Often the problems can be overcome by careful siting of these items, though it may prove necessary to call in an expert to fit suppression devices to the offending equipment.

Decca and Loran

These are both radio navigation aids that calculate the boat's position from signals received from a chain of shore-based transmitters. Their basic principles of operation are essentially the same, but Loran has a longer range at the expense of some accuracy. Loran covers the USA and Mediterranean, whilst Decca Navigator covers North European waters.

As both types of set display the position in latitude and longitude, often to one hundredth of a nautical mile, it is all too easy to follow Decca or Loran blindly. This is made all the more tempting by the possibility of entering waypoints, with the course and distance to the next waypoint being calculated by the set. One must always bear in mind that, although the accuracy can be within 50 yards (50 m) in the centre of a chain in good conditions, this can increase to a mile or so at long range at twilight, and the signals can be severely distorted or completely masked out by a large headland. Furthermore, there will always be a difference in position when changing between chains, as the errors in the system are not constant throughout. Thus, one should always keep an eye on the displays giving data such as which chain is in use, the strength of the signals and the likely accuracy of the fix. In addition, one should always plot one's position on the chart, just as one would with any other position-fixing system, and cross check it against one's DR.

Decca does not make the navigator redundant by any means, though it does change his role significantly. As he (or she) has to spend less time working out where the boat is, he can now concentrate on finding the best route from A to B. As far as Decca is concerned, this means comparing the Decca fix and the estimated position to find out whether the tides are running as predicted in the tidal atlas, and using this information to work out a course to steer to the next waypoint, allowing for the expected tides and weather conditions along the leg. If one just followed the course given by the Decca set one would sail a considerably greater distance than if one sailed the correct compass course for the leg, unless the tide was running parallel to the course to the next waypoint.

Satnav

Satnav, and its eventual replacement GPS (Global Positioning System), use signals picked up from orbiting satellites instead of land-based transmitters, and a fix is obtained when a satellite is overhead, normally every hour or so. As one would expect, coverage is worldwide, though some parts of the world are better covered than others.

Satnav is not as popular as Decca Navigator because most people confine their sailing to one area, and if that is covered by Decca or Loran they prefer the continuously updated fix that these systems give. For example, if the accuracy of the Decca is first cross-checked with a good compass fix, one can tack in and out along a rocky shore (should one wish to do so) using Decca, whereas due to the long interval between fixes with Satnav this is clearly impossible.

Sextant

The sextant is perhaps not used as much as it should be for navigation these days. Astro navigation has a name for being a complex subject, so many owners have steered clear of the area and bought Decca or Satnav instead. In fact, with a little practice, the necessary calculations can be done in five or ten minutes with a pocket calculator and tables, or in even less time if one invests in one of the pre-programmed navigational calculators that are available. Also, it is not necessary to learn all the stars, as the almanac can recommend six or seven stars which will provide a good fix. Knowing roughly where he is from his dead reckoning, the navigator works out where the stars will be, takes the sights, and then plots the position lines.

The sextant is not just an instrument for offshore use. For example, even if you can only pick out one feature of known height on a coastline, by taking a compass bearing and measuring the angle between the top and base of the object with a sextant, you can calculate your position. When all is said and done, however, the sextant is dependant on good visibility in just the same way as the hand bearing compass is.

VHF radio

For those who have done their homework and know how to get the best out of VHF, it is invaluable. It offers intership and ship-to-shore radio communication at ranges of up to about 20 miles and 60 miles respectively. Figure 4.5 shows a typical set suitable for a yacht.

The most common uses are liaisons between yachts, calling up marinas to book a berth for the night, and linking in to the

telephone system through a coast radio station to keep in contact with home or office. The coastguard, port authorities and coast radio stations broadcast a wide range of other extremely useful information. This includes weather forecasts, Decca and navigational warnings, shipping movements. Perhaps most importantly, VHF is a means of calling up the rescue services that is considerably more versatile than setting off a flare. In addition, race committees help competitors by broadcasting information such as sail numbers of boats over the line. Moreover, by judicious eavesdropping it is often possible to discover the latitude and longitude of marks that are being laid.

Finally, over the last few years a number of 'radio lighthouses' have been set up. Once the identification signal of the required station has been received, one counts the number of pulses till the tone changes and then looks up the bearing from the transmitter in a table. Although obviously of limited range, this is considerably easier to use than RDF, and accurate to about two degrees.

Charts and books

The most basic requirement when navigating is a good selection of charts. First of all, there should ideally be one chart covering the entire passage. Secondly, there should be enough detailed charts to cover all the coastal work, so that the boat can close the shore without fear of hazards omitted from the large scale chart and can also find a safe harbour or anchorage should the need arise. These detailed charts also give much more tidal stream data, so they help one to work the tides on passage. In my view, it is impossible to carry too many charts, as all too often the navigator finds that an extra chart or two would have proved useful.

As well as the standard British or American charts, it is often useful to have others produced by the country in whose waters you are sailing – or, if the country was once a colony, the charts of the erstwhile ruling power – as these often show much greater detail, though some discrepancies are bound to be found between the surveys of different hydrographic offices. As all chart symbols follow the same international standard, there should be little problem in using these charts.

If Decca or Loran is carried, special charts overprinted with the Decca or Loran lattice may be useful, and some countries publish charts giving data on known fixed errors. Although generally not strictly necessary on board, as most sets give a read-out of latitude and longitude, the study of lattice charts helps to identify areas where the fixes are likely to be poor: for example, where only two out of the three slave stations can be received, or where the 'lanes' are nearly parallel, or at the limit of the range of a given chain of stations.

In addition to charts, a great deal of information concerning tides and currents, navigational buoys and lights, coast radio stations, weather forecasts, RDF beacons and navigational warnings is required. There are two schools of thought on the best source of such information: an almanac, such as Reed's or Macmillan's, containing all the above data plus much else of use to the yachtsman; or Admiralty publications, such as the Tidal Stream Atlases, List of Lights and List of Radio Signals. Whilst having everything in one book is often simpler and cheaper, the Admiralty publications often contain more detailed information and, more importantly, they can be updated weekly by Notices to Mariners. Thus, for serious extended cruising it is often preferable to have the Admiralty publications.

In addition, where a sextant is carried the boat will require a nautical almanac, giving astronomical data for the year, and a set of sight reduction tables. A number of these are available, but my preference is for *Sight Reduction Tables for Air Navigation* (Publication HO 249), as it covers the whole world in only three volumes and also tells you which stars are most suitable to use at a given date and place.

Preparation is the key

As the amount of space, and often time, available to the navigator is generally fairly limited, the best approach is for him to do as much of the navigation as possible in the comfort of his home. Then, hopefully, most of what he does on board will simply be a matter of checking off progress against his planned route.

Once the cruising area or race area is known, a lot of the preparation is simply gathering all the available data in a more usable form. The two most basic factors are the weather and the tides. Thus if a list is made of all available weather forecasts in sequence, together with the radio frequency and the area covered, it is easy to find when the next weather forecast will be broadcast. Sources are listed in some nautical almanacs, and include both national and local radio stations, coastguard stations, and coast radio stations. Clearly the usefulness of the different forecasts varies quite widely, depending upon whom they are aimed at, but some broadcasts, especially those of local radio stations, give very detailed forecasts for inshore areas.

As far as the tides are concerned, one can look up the times and heights of tides at all the standard and secondary ports that are used in the tidal atlases and charts that cover your area, and mark them accordingly in terms of the local time that will be used on board (eg BST, GMT, etc). From the heights of high and low water one can determine whether the tides are springs or neaps. Also, you can work out the times at which one can get over any bars or shallows at the entrance to harbours, or the times at which lock gates are open. It is also worth looking at all the detailed charts of headlands or bays, as they often show the tidal streams in considerably more detail than the tidal stream atlases. If comparing charts produced by different publishers, you may be quite surprised how greatly they sometimes vary regarding tidal strengths and times of slack water.

Moving on to aids to navigation, another list can be made of RDF beacons and VHF radio lighthouses in the area, with range, Morse identification signals and frequencies. Some of the commercially produced chartlets showing the RDF beacons are particularly useful in this respect.

Route planning

The extent to which the route can be planned in advance depends largely on how much information you have as to where you are going. If the race has a fixed course or your cruise has a fixed itinerary, a great deal more planning can be done than if the course is first displayed at the start or you want to cruise down the Brittany coast, but will let the weather decide your plans for you.

If you know when and where you are going, the job is relatively straightforward. First of all, pick out the positions of any headlands or marks that have to be rounded, either on the most direct route or on a beat, where you are sailing at 45 or 50 degrees to the rhumb line. Then, work out the course to steer between these points, allowing for the tide. Note that, although it may be easier for the navigator to keep the boat sailing along the rhumb line for a leg, the boat may, in fact, be sailing further through the water. This is because, in keeping to the rhumb line across changing tidal streams, boat speed is wasted in unnecessarily countering the effects of the tide.

It is well worth plotting one's expected position for every few hours of the journey. By comparing the boat's predicted position with the tidal stream atlas, you will see if there are any tidal 'gates' around headlands, and if there are any areas of strong tide that it would be particularly advantageous to get into or steer clear of.

It is often the case when cruising that you know where you want to go, but are fairly flexible about the time of departure or arrival. Then, once the rhumb line has been drawn on the chart it pays to study the tidal atlas and see at what times you will get a fair tide round major headlands. Having decided upon the times at which you want to arrive at each of these tidal 'gates', if necessary comparing them to get an advantageous tide round as many headlands as possible, you can work backwards to get the best time of departure. If it is impossible to avoid a foul tide at one or other of a pair of headlands, this might be a good excuse to discover another anchorage!

Navigation on board

Assuming that there was time to do all the necessary preparation, the navigation when actually sailing should be relatively simple: just a matter of taking a fix every so often and checking the position against the expected track. Initially, you will not need to take a fix very often, and changes in course will be relatively small. But as you approach a waypoint you will need to fix your position more frequently until the waypoint is identified.

It is a good idea to lay out your charts and other information properly before the voyage. The large-scale charts of the point of departure should be at the top, together with a chart covering the entire sailing area. Then should come any detailed charts of headlands or other hazards *en route*, and finally the large-scale charts of the destination. Times of radio transmissions, etc can either be posted by the chart table or kept in a waterproof notebook.

One problem, increasingly pertinent for navigators of even quite small craft, is how to decide which of the many position-fixing systems to use in a given set of circumstances. For ease of use, Decca or Loran score just about every time. However, they are not always accurate, and accuracy should be checked both by using the set's own indicators and by looking at factors such as how far one is from the stations, at what angle the lanes cross each other (the more nearly perpendicular to one another they are, the better the fix) and if there is any likelihood of distortion, such as if you are sailing in a bay surrounded by very high cliffs. Also, the system should be checked periodically against another fixing method, ideally a compass fix. Any errors will be more or less fixed over quite a large area, and on some sets you can input an error correction.

Often, if reception is poor, it may pay to select a different pair of slave stations or, if near the boundary of a chain, to use the adjoining one.

Compass fixes are the most reliable, assuming that you know what landmark or light you are taking a bearing on and you can find three objects at angles of about 60 degrees to each other. Conditions must also be calm enough for the compass to stay fairly steady while you take the fix. Unfortunately, these conditions are not always met, especially when sailing offshore.

Until the advent of Satnav and Decca, radio direction finding was the standard means of position-fixing when a visual fix was not possible. It is generally good enough for reasonably accurate navigation, but should not be relied on close inshore or in tricky waters, as even in ideal conditions the errors can be two degrees each side of the actual bearing. Large errors are possible due to a poor signal or a signal that crosses the land at a shallow angle. With RDF, remember not to use a station if you are outside its quoted range and wherever possible to select stations so that the signal crosses at right angles to the shore, with no headlands or other obstructions in the way. Whenever possible one should switch to a visual fix or some other means of navigation.

Finally, we have the sextant. It is used little by yachtsmen these days, due to the supposed complexity of the calculations required. This is something of a myth, though, as the sums can easily be done in five or ten minutes with a set of tables and a pocket calculator. Alternatively, calculators and computers can be bought with all the data and calculations programmed into them, which makes life even easier. Using a sextant generally produces a position line almost as good as a visual bearing, though for astro navigation the sky needs to be clear enough to see the body you are taking a sight on.

The navigator is also responsible for gathering and interpreting a whole mass of information concerning wind, tide, shipping, etc. In the immediate sphere of the boat, this information is largely gathered by direct observation: looking at the clouds, seeing the tide on moored boats and buoys, and so on. This must then be tied in with more general information, gathered from the radio, charts and tidal atlases. Similarly, when very close inshore the boat is generally piloted by eye, using either local knowledge or a chart in the cockpit. Where necessary this is augmented with the echo sounder, a hand-bearing compass or a Decca fix.

As the boat sails further offshore, there is less need for constant position-fixing, and greater use is made of first the compass, and then RDF or Decca. Also the emphasis changes from immediate tactical problems like running aground, rounding the mark or negotiating the harbour entrance to more strategic ones like deciding which side of the rhumb line to go for the fastest or most comfortable passage, and when best to tack to take advantage of the turn of the tide or the approaching weather system.

This is not to say that when sailing offshore tactical considerations are disregarded. Similarly, the general strategy must be borne in mind when sailing close inshore, but the navigator must always obtain the correct balance between the immediate and the longer-term considerations, and also use the appropriate tools for the job.

Beating

On a beat the question of which tack is favoured is often a vexed one: Other things being equal, it pays to do the longer tack first. The logic behind this is that if the wind frees you will be able to lay the next mark without tacking, and if you are headed you will be on the favoured side of the rhumb line. However, things are seldom equal. It may pay to choose one side of the leg to benefit from an advantageous tidal stream. Alternatively, it may take you into smoother water, which will improve your speed quite considerably, especially if the wind is light (this point is often forgotten, but it is particularly important with small boats that are stopped relatively easily in a seaway).

The change of tide will effectively change the wind direction and strength to some extent. The change in wind speed is relatively unimportant, but the shift in direction can be quite useful. If the tide is coming from under the lee bow the apparent wind is freer letting you point up higher than you could if there was no tide running. Thus, there is a slight benefit to be had in tacking when the tide turns, so that it stays under your lee bow. However, this effect diminishes the closer you are sailing to the direction of the tidal streams and as your boat speed increases in relation to the strength of the tidal stream.

The importance of windshifts cannot be overemphasised. Even if one side of the leg is clearly favoured, in most cases it will pay to watch the wind and tack on the major shifts while edging towards the favoured side, rather than sailing straight to the favoured side and then straight for the mark. A five degree windshift is equivalent to a ten per cent increase in boatspeed; or if you are sailing at five knots it corresponds to dodging half a knot of tide.

Although there is generally a favoured side of the beat due to conditions of wind or tide, it very seldom pays to go right out on a limb as whilst a further windshift or a change in windspeed may act in your favour, experience has shown that the likelihood is that you will miss the tide gate round the headland, or as soon as you tack to lay the mark the wind will head you by 40 degrees. The way to avoid being caught out like this is to draw a cone from objective on the chart with sides about 20 or 30 degrees off the true wind direction, and then make sure you stay within the cone unless you have a very good reason to do otherwise. The angle between the sides of the cone may vary depending on the conditions: in very shifty winds it is safest to stay close to the rhumb line; in steady conditions there is no harm in wandering some distance off to either side. If there is a strong cross tide or weather reports indicate a wind shift further along the leg, you may well want to twist the cone round so as to stay uptide of the target, or to ensure that you are in position to make the most of the windshift when it arrives.

The exception is in very light winds when the sails barely fill and everyone except those actually racing is either sunbathing or motoring home. In these conditions it often pays to go miles off course to find flatter water or a zephyr of wind – for example, a thermal wind round a steep headland or a land breeze close inshore at night.

Running
All too often when running the crew simply put up the spinnaker or cruising chute and head straight for their

destination. However, once again the aim is to optimise the VMG, and it is very seldom that this is achieved by sailing in a straight line. This is because as one heads up from a dead run the apparent wind speed increases, and so there is effectively more wind to push you along. Even for a dyed-in-the-wool cruising man this has advantages: heading up slightly will often damp any rolling tendencies, making the ride more comfortable. Once again, the question is how far to head up, but this time the angle is far less critical than it was when beating. In light winds boat speed increases greatly for a small increase in apparent wind, and so it may pay to tack down the run as much as 40 degrees off the straight line course. As the wind pipes up there is less and less room for improvement in boat speed, and once the boat is travelling at maximum speed there is no benefit in tacking downwind. The sail plan also has an effect on the optimum course to steer downwind, as genoas and cruising chutes are relatively inefficient on a dead run, even if poled out to windward, and so it generally pays to sail a lower course when these sails are set than when a spinnaker is carried.

As when sailing on the wind, the effects of wind shifts and tidal conditions must be borne in mind, as must the likely smoothness of the water. In light airs it will always pay to go for flat water, but in a breeze heading for more exposed waters may well result in higher surfing speeds.

Reaching

A reach is in many ways the easiest course to sail, with the helmsman simply steering a straight-line course and the crew trimming the sails as necessary. The main trick here is for the helmsman to compensate adequately for when he bears off in a puff. In stronger winds it is very easy to keep bearing off when overpowered in the gusts and not luff up enough in the lulls, particularly if the wind is rising and you are trying to get by without tucking a reef in!

In the same way as the boat's polar curve diagram (fig 4.6) gives the optimum tacking and gybing angles, it also shows when it pays to put the spinnaker up: too early, and it just pulls you sideways; but too late, and the genoa quickly loses its drive. There is often, in fact, a slight hollow in the polar curve

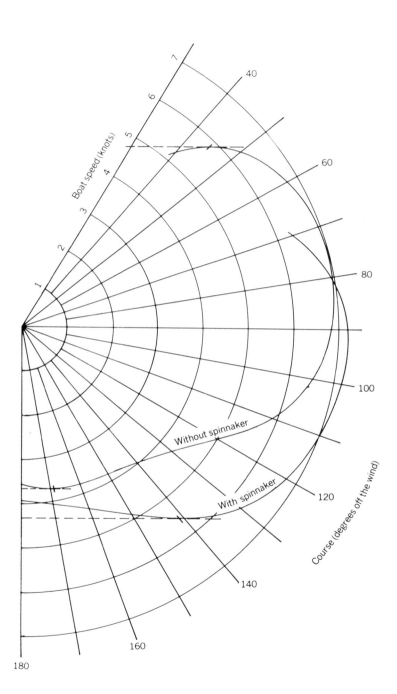

Boat speed (knots)

40

60

80

100

120

140

160

180

Course (degrees off the wind)

Without spinnaker

With spinnaker

Fig 4.6 *Polar curve diagram, showing relative speed on different points of sailing, with and without spinnaker. In this example, the optimum course on a beating leg would be about 45 degrees off the wind. On a running leg it would be about 141 degrees with spinnaker, and 169 without.*

at the change-over point (at about 81 degrees in fig 4.6), and so if you are sailing a course close to the change-over point it will pay to sail high and hold on to the genoa for part of the leg, then bear off slightly and set the spinnaker for the remainder. However, cruising chutes are more efficient on a shy reach than spinnakers and so they lack this inflection in the curve.

On a reaching leg, the navigator's job is relatively simple. He must periodically fix the boat's position, see how it compares with that anticipated, then order any necessary course change. This should be done along the entire leg, as a small change made early on is much easier and much more efficient than a major change of course at the last minute. When planning the leg, it is a good idea to aim slightly upwind of the destination, so that one does not end up beating up to it, often against the tide. The only exception is in very light airs when tidal conditions predominate, in which case one should aim to arrive uptide of one's destination. The amount of room to leave for error depends largely on the accuracy of one's navigation, but it is always a good idea to aim for a powerfully lit buoy or a prominent headland, so that in the final stages of the leg it is easy to home-in on the objective.

5

COASTAL SAILING

The vast majority of production boats are designed with a bias very much towards weekend sailing – together with the occasional extended cruise along the coast or short sea crossing – and without doubt this is the use to which most boats are put.

The design requirements for coastal work are essentially those met by compromising sailing performance with ease of handling and good accommodation, but this may still result in a number of different styles of design. They vary from heavy traditional cruising boats through to sporty lightweight designs with nearly plumb bows and wide powerful sterns. Each one represents the designer's and builder's combined efforts to find a hole in the market.

On the construction and fitting-out side, knowing that the boat will be sailing in reasonably sheltered waters for fairly short lengths of time, with good back-up facilities ashore, leads to the temptation to reduce the thickness of the laminate or the size of the fittings, to be able to sell the boat at a lower price than the competition. For example, most cruising boats carry winches smaller than their racing counterparts, and yet the average family crew is not as strong and fit as a racing crew should be. The extent to which designers and builders have succumbed to this temptation varies from one design to another, but one should always bear the possibility in mind when looking for a boat. Talking to surveyors and reading the more comprehensive reviews in sailing magazines will give you some idea of the quality of the hull structure, and comparing the standard of fittings can easily be done between one boat and another.

The sail plan

I think it is true to say that most new boats in this size range are designed with a fractional rig unless they are a continuation of a well-established design, or they have a gaff or junk rig to create a special style of boat. The arguments for a fractional rig in this size of boat are so numerous that it is not really worth considering masthead rig.

Advantages of the fractional rig

On the performance front, the fractional rig is much faster reaching, and only loses out to a masthead rig running dead downwind in light airs or beating in a lumpy sea. Also, fewer headsails need to be carried, the small spinnaker and genoas are easier to control, and sail can easily be reduced by reefing the mainsail – a much easier operation than a headsail change. In the size of boat we are dealing with, there are no structural problems with a fractional rig, and the swept-back spreaders obviate any need for the complexities of runners. A fractional rig also helps down below: the mast generally comes at the aft end of the forward berths, leaving a large uncluttered saloon, whereas on a masthead rigged boat it would come considerably further aft. Finally, there is the styling consideration: it must be admitted that, as most racing boats carry fractional rigs, putting one on a cruiser gives it a more sporty image.

Headsails

An increasing number of designers carry the idea of small headsails one step further, by adopting a self-tacking jib. This is much easier to use when sailing with a young or inexperienced crew, as the sail looks after itself when the boat tacks. However, the jibsheet track must really extend right outboard if the sail is to set properly on a reach. Moreover, unless the mainsail area or the height of the rig has been increased to compensate for the smaller foresail, the boat may prove a bit sluggish in light airs.

Rather than carry a large number of genoas or go to the expense of roller reefing gear, the cruising yachtsman can use reefing genoas. These may either have a reef cringle on the luff as well as the leech or use the same tack cringle as the full-sized sail, with just the clew being reefed. If the tack is reefed as well as the clew, a greater reduction in sail area can be achieved. However, if just the clew is reefed, the resulting high clew gives a better-shaped sail for reaching, with a leech that hooks up less to windward. In either case, there must be reef points along the sail to stop the reefed part dragging in the water and becoming damaged. As it can be very difficult to thread a light line through an eye in the sail, permanently attached reef points are best.

Downwind sails

As far as downwind sails are concerned, the choice lies between a spinnaker and a cruising chute. With the size of sails that we are dealing with, the spinnaker is small enough to be easily handled, and so one can choose the sails on a performance basis as much as on manageability.

On a close reach the cruising chute is set with its luff pretty tight, and acts like a large full genoa, whereas the extra fullness of the spinnaker makes the sail tighter-leeched, heeling the boat over more and largely counteracting the thrust from the front half of the sail. As soon as the spinnaker pole can be pulled back off the forestay, the extra area and fullness of the spinnaker gives it a considerable edge over the cruising chute. Furthermore, as the pole comes aft it brings the sail out of the lee of the mainsail into clear air. In fact, on a dead run a cruising chute set to leeward sets very poorly indeed and it should really be poled out to windward like a spinnaker.

When running, both spinnakers and cruising chutes would be more efficient if set with a longer spinnaker pole, as this would pull the sail further out of the influence of the mainsail. Although a longer pole would effectively prevent a dip-pole gybe, there is no problem in doing an end-for-end gybe on boats of this size.

Cruising chutes

Cruising chutes offer much improved downwind performance over a genoa, and although it cannot match a spinnaker in performance this is made up for by its ease of handling.

The tack of the sail is fastened at the stem, and it is hoisted on a spinnaker halyard. The sheet is led to the rail, as with a normal genoa. When close reaching, which is the forte of this sail, the halyard is set up tight and the sail sheeted in like a genoa. As the boat bears off, the sail is made fuller by easing out the halyard along with the sheet (as the sail is often set in light airs the sheet does not want to be too large and heavy). When the boat is close to a dead run, the sail will be blanketed by the mainsail and tend to collapse, since there is no spinnaker pole to swing the sail to weather. Once the boat is on a dead run, the sail can be goosewinged, and it will fly much more stably with the clew poled out to weather.

There are a wide variety of cuts and sizes of cruising chute, derived from designs for genoas, spinnakers and bloopers. Although a cross-cut sail will be cheapest, addition of radial-cut corners to the sail means that the loads are spread out from the corners much more efficiently, and there is less likelihood of the sail distorting when set in a breeze.

Setting up the cruising rig

The majority of cruising boats will either be masthead rigged, or fractional rigged with aft-swept spreaders. In both cases the aim is to set the mast up so that it is well supported and yet can bend sufficiently to allow some control over the shape of the mainsail.

Once the mast has been stepped the first necessity is to ensure that it has the correct fore-and-aft rake. A small amount of rake aft seems to make most boats sail at their best, but the exact amount depends on the boat and the sails. Now check that the mast is not leaning to one side, by using a cleated halyard to check the distance from the hounds down to the chainplates on each side. The mast should be set up first with the slack just taken out of the upper shrouds (caps), and all the lower and intermediate shrouds slack. Now tighten up the uppers, and then do the same with the lowers and intermediates, checking that the mast remains straight by sighting up the luff groove from the gooseneck.

Now it is time to go out sailing, ideally in a Force Three so that the boat is fairly well pressed under full mainsail and number-one genoa. On the wind, the leeward upper shroud should only be just slack. Once the uppers have been tensioned enough to achieve this, the lowers and intermediates should be tensioned so that the mast remains straight athwartships (once more, sight up the luff of the mainsail to check this). Now, if the backstay is not readily adjustable while sailing, it needs to be tensioned so as to minimise forestay sag. The sag can be assessed by sighting up the luff of the genoa, and you will see that beyond a certain point increasing the backstay tension has little effect. Now go back and check the fore-and-aft bend of the mast, and if this is too much for the cut of the mainsail you will need to increase the tension of the lowers slightly.

With a fractional rig the tension in the upper shrouds generally needs to be greater than with a masthead rig, as if the leeward shroud is allowed to go slack the mast can swing about the weather spreader and pump excessively in a seaway. Also, with the lee shroud slack, the pull of the forestay when the boat is on the wind will tend to pull the mast forwards, greatly increasing the amount of sag in the genoa luff. Thus, in most fractionally rigged boats the rigging should be set up much tighter than is generally the case. Do not be alarmed if you cannot easily tighten the turnbuckle in harbour, but have to tighten it when sailing by tightening up the leeward rigging on each tack. Although the backstay does help to tighten the forestay, it also induces a lot of bend in the top of the mast. If the backstay is used excessively the mainsail will be either too full in the head in light airs or too flat in a blow.

Once the rig has been set up, one should sight up the mast and check it periodically. The rigging, and in some cases the hull, slowly stretches during the season – particularly early on in the season – and the rigging will have to be adjusted periodically to allow for this.

Deck layout
The key to designing a deck layout is to keep everything as simple as is functionally possible. This is particularly so on a cruising boat, as the crew do not want to spend all their time adjusting the rig. Furthermore, having too many fittings both adds to the expense and clutters up the decks. This is seldom a problem with production cruisers, though, as the majority of builders cut the deck fittings to the minimum, in order to keep the initial cost of the boat low. One can easily add extra fittings to a boat, so long as they do not have to be on part of the deck with a foam or balsa core, and one has access to the underside

of the deck. Most builders are happy to upgrade the specification of winches or other fittings when you order a new boat.

Halyards

Assuming the crew consists of at least three persons, the halyards are best led aft to the cockpit, along with the reef lines. Although these lines clutter up the coachroof top, the problem can be solved by sacrificing a bit of headroom and running the lines in a trough covered by a removable panel (it must be removable so that lines can be replaced or re-rove easily). With the reef lines led aft to a winch other than the main halyard winch, the person operating the halyard can also wind in the reef lines. The lines can either be made fast at the winch, or on a stopper at the forward end of the boom by the crewman who is working at the mast. A stopper is ideal for the reef lines, as it means that one does not need to fit two winches specifically for reefing.

In the foretriangle, the boat needs either two halyards that can both double for the genoa and the spinnaker, or two genoa halyards and one spinnaker halyard. Normal polyester ropes are generally too elastic for halyards and wire is hard on the crew's hands, so Kevlar is the obvious choice. This does not have the same short life expectancy as Kevlar sails, and so is perfectly acceptable for cruising boats, but the sheaves do need to be slightly larger in diameter than would be the case for polyester. Once again, the halyards are best led aft to the cockpit. Where possible the two genoa halyards need to be led to the opposite side of the cockpit to the spinnaker halyard, so that one does not end up wanting to put two lines round one winch when changing between headsail and spinnaker.

Hanks, headfoil or roller reefing?

For the genoa, one has the choice between jib hanks, a headfoil and a furling genoa. Hanks have the great advantage that the sail cannot blow overboard when being set or lowered. A headsail change need not take much longer than with a headfoil: the bowman clips the new sail onto the forestay, secures the tack and attaches the new halyard; the cockpit crew lowers the old sail, and as it comes down the hanks are taken off; as soon as the last one is off, the new sail can be hoisted. Hanks are also preferable if the boat is trailed often, as the mast is much easier to raise or drop if there is only a wire forestay.

A headfoil makes sail changes faster, as the new sail can be hoisted up before the old one is lowered. Moreover there is no sag between the hanks when the halyard tension is eased to make the sail fuller. Against this, a second pair of hands is often required to gather the sail when it is lowered, and in the long term plastic headfoils become brittle with exposure to the sunlight.

Finally, there are furling headsails. These make it very easy to reef the sail from the cockpit, with none of the crew required on the foredeck. Unfortunately, as the sail is reefed it becomes increasingly full in the middle, and less efficient when sailing to windward. Some sailmakers put a layer of foam up the luff to take the fullness out as the sail is furled, but this solution is not perfect. Also, if the sail is left furled when the boat is not in use, the leech and foot disintegrate much quicker than the rest of the sail, due to their being left exposed to the sunlight. This can be avoided by having a sacrificial strip of cloth sewn along the edges of the sail, or a cover can be pulled up over the sail when the boat is on her moorings. However, when all is said and done, a furling genoa is seldom worthwhile on a boat of this size, as the sails are small enough for one or two crew to handle without any problems.

Genoa sheets

The genoa tracks really want to be eight or ten degrees off the centreline (which means that for every 10 ft (3.04 m) aft of the stem fitting, the tracks should be 17 to 21 in (43 to 53 cm) off the centreline). But this is seldom possible on a cruising boat due to the width of the coachroof, unless the tracks are mounted on top of the coachroof. The other limiting factor for the number-one and number-two genoas is the width of the staying base and the spreader length. A wider staying base gives more support to the mast, and also often lets the chainplates be moved outboard of the saloon settee berths. Having one long track for all genoas avoids problems of having to move fairleads between tracks because replacement sails have different clew heights. If the tracks do not have endstops the cars can be easily slid on from either end, to suit whichever sail is being set next. (Sliding them on with the sheave aft of the locating pin makes adjusting the lead with the sail set much easier, as the sheet is clear of the pin.) Some care needs to be paid to the siting of the track for the number-three jib. Often, to get the correct sheeting angle on the wind, it will need to be positioned so that the sheet leads inboard of the shrouds, or between the cap and lower shrouds. However, when the boat bears off and the sheet is eased, it will tend to foul the shrouds. Thus, it may be worth fitting a second track outboard of the shrouds for use when reaching, or siting the track far enough outboard to avoid this problem.

The genoa sheet will lead back to the winch either directly or via a turning block. Whichever is the case, the rope wants to lead in to the winch from slightly below the level of the drum, so as to avoid riding turns. There should be at least 18 in (46 cm) between the winch and the final block, so that any twists can work themselves out of the rope. The winch may be either on the cockpit coaming or, if the boat has a small cockpit, sited at the aft end of the coachroof. Wherever it is located, there needs to be an absolute minimum clearance of 12 in (30 cm) for the handle to swing in. As most cruising boats sacrifice some cockpit length to a larger interior, there can be numerous obstructions that interfere with the winches – the coachroof or guardrails, a spray dodger, the mainsheet (especially when let off for sailing downwind), or even the helmsman! Any one of these can make handling the winch difficult.

When tacking, the life of the crew can be made much easier if the helmsman slows down the tack towards the end. The load quickly comes off the 'old sheet and the sail is blown round the mast, but, if the helmsman then slows down and holds the boat slightly high of a close-hauled course, the crew can sheet in the genoa before the full load comes onto the sheet.

Spinnaker sheets

For the spinnaker the halyard will be led aft out of the mast at deck level just as for the genoa, but at the hounds the halyard will pass through a fairlead or crane so that it can take the sideways pull of the sail without jumping off the mast sheave. Ideally, the halyard should emerge from the mast about 6 or 7 ft (1.8 or 2.1 m) above deck level, so that the crew can help hoist the sail by pulling down on the halyard at the mast.

On deck, the sheets will be led round turning blocks mounted right aft on the quarters, and then forwards to the sheet winches. Then, there may be a pair of permanently rigged guys, led round sheaves positioned close to the point of maximum beam, but if possible not in a position where they will bend a stanchion on a shy reach. Alternatively, a pair of 'tweakers' will be fitted. These consist of a floating block on each sheet, led through a turning block where the guy would normally be and aft to a strong cleat. If permanent guys are fitted there is a bit more string on the boat, but gybing is easier for the foredeck hand as he can clip the lazy guy onto the spinnaker pole and the pole onto the mast without any load on it. With the tweakers, the cockpit crew pull down the windward tweaker so that the sheet becomes the guy, and so the pole is always attached to a line under load when gybing. The helmsman must keep the boat running square until the pole is properly clipped onto the mast if the foredeck hand's job is to be made easy. When running in a breeze, the tweaker can be pulled down on the leeward side or the sail sheeted by the lazy guy, so as to close the spinnaker leech and steady the sail.

As the spinnaker and genoa will probably both be set together when changing sails, the boat will need either two sheet winches on each side of the cockpit or a clam cleat between the turning block and the winch, so that the spinnaker or the genoa sheet can be secured without occupying a winch.

Mainsheet
On most boats the mainsheet is lead from half-way along the boom. It may then be brought straight down to the cockpit floor, or to a traveller. When sailing on the wind, if a traveller is used, the sheet itself just controls the fullness of the sail and the tightness of the leech, while the traveller controls the angle of the sail to the centreline. Unfortunately, for maximum efficiency the traveller needs to be as high up as possible and to run the full width of the boat, and this clearly creates a major obstacle when crossing the cockpit. Thus, on a cruising boat it

generally pays to have just a short traveller across the middle of the cockpit, and a powerful kicking strap which can be led back to a small winch if necessary.

On some boats the sheet is led from the aft end of the boom, and down to the transom. With this sytem a powerful kicking strap is essential, as even if there is a track its arc of travel will be relatively small. Also, if the sheet slopes forwards there may be a tendency for it to catch the helmsman's head when gybing, especially if he (or she) sits right aft, as is the case with a rudder hung on the transom.

Winches

Next, a word on the winches themselves. These are often under-sized on production boats, as a means of cutting costs. Table 5.1 shows the minimum size of winch that should be used for a given purpose. For the rope to have the best grip on the drum, light alloy anodized drums are to be preferred. The one exception is if wire halyards will pass round the winch, in which case stainless steel should be used, but this should be avoided if possible, as a rope-to-wire splice can be damaged if it passes round a winch drum regularly. Self-tailing winches, though considerably more expensive, make it much easier for a small crew to work the boat as one crew member can do the work of two. They are at their most useful as halyard and reef winches. A small but important point is that the boat must have enough winch handle pockets, sited close enough to the winches to be useful. Even lock-in handles can be flicked out by a stray sheet, and my preference is to use the simpler and cheaper plain handles, always remembering to put them back in their pockets after use.

Keel designs

Whilst the racing yachtsman will nearly always go for a deep fin keel for maximum efficiency and the offshore cruiser will probably also have a fin or long keel, of slightly greater area, the typical cruising boat that spends much of its time in coastal waters will benefit from a shallow-draft or lifting keel.

A lifting keel may be either of the daggerboard type or a centreboard. The centreboard is often designed so that it will

Table 5.1   Recommended winch sizes for different sail areas
Minimum winch ratios (:1)

Mainsail

	Sail area					
(Sq ft)	97	161	183	226	237	280
(Sq m)	9	15	17	21	22	26
Halyard	6	7	18	30	30	40
Sheet	NA	6	7	16	24	30
Reefing	6	6	7	7	10	18

Genoa

	Sail area				
(Sq ft)	194	226	258	323	366
(Sq m)	18	21	24	30	34
Halyard	6	7	8	18	30
Sheet	7	8	18	30	40
Runners	7	7	8	16	16

Spinnaker

(Sq ft)	237	301	431	603	797
(Sq m)	22	28	40	56	74
Halyard	6	6	7	16	24
Sheet	NA	6	7	16	30

come up on touching the bottom, thus reducing the strains on the boat and also giving the helmsman the chance to turn around before the boat goes hard aground. The daggerboard is generally more intrusive inside the boat, but it does have the advantage of potentially greater strength if the boat is pushed beam-on to an obstruction.

Unfortunately, both types reduce the stability of the boat, since the ballast cannot be placed as low down as one would wish. The situation can be improved to some extent by fitting a stub keel to house the board, and this also gives a very strong structure for the boat to dry out on.

If a fixed keel is fitted, it may just be a long shallow fin keel. This gives low draft without the drawbacks of a lifting keel, plus exceptionally good directional stability, and the drop in windward performance is not too great. However, the boat still needs support when drying out if she is not to fall on her side. This problem can be overcome by bilge keels, which are ideal for cruising in shallow waters as one can simply let the boat sit on the bottom as the tide goes out, have a meal or sleep, and then carry on sailing when the water returns. The price to be paid though, is in lost performance due to the weather bilge keel being so close to the surface. Also, as with the shallow-draft fin keel, there is some reduction in stability and increase in wetted surface area.

The stability problem can be overcome in a number of ways. The simplest of these is a bulb or Scheel keel, where the fatter tip section move the centre of gravity lower. Wings do the same, and if properly designed they also increase the efficiency of the keel. Alternatively, the higher centre of gravity can be accepted, and compensated for by a smaller rig or more internal ballast.

Another problem with shallow keel configurations is that the depth of the rudder must also be reduced, as otherwise the boat will sit on her rudder when taking the ground. This reduces the efficiency of the rudder, and the blade also comes out of the water more quickly as the boat heels. On a transom-mounted rudder, the blade can be deep in normal use, and then raised in its own small daggerboard case when entering shallow water. Alternatively, some boats are being fitted with two rudders, like a pair of bilge keels, so that the leeward rudder is always fully immersed, and sometimes the boat can also sit on her rudders when drying out.

Trailer sailing

With small boats, 'trailer sailing' can offer an ideal solution to the problem of where to keep the boat. However, its success depends upon the ease with which the boat can be loaded onto and launched off the trailer. Some well-thought-out boats have a custom-designed trailer and are designed especially for frequent launch and recovery operations, the Dehlya range being a good example. First of all, the mast is stepped on deck in a tabernacle for easy raising and lowering, whilst the centreboard can be raised and lowered from on deck using a standard winch handle and the rudder assembly drops into a locating hole in the cockpit floor. Secondly, the boat sits on a launching trolley on top of the road trailer, and so to launch the boat the trailer is parked at the water's edge, with only the launching trolley going into the water, thereby ensuring that the trailer bearings stay dry and salt-free. Once the boat is launched, a self-flooding ballast tank fills up, increasing the boat's displacement to give good stability when sailing, but as the tank is emptied when the boat comes ashore the towing weight is kept as low as possible. Furthermore, because many trailer sailers are bought by first time buyers on a relatively tight budget, the boats are sold in a very basic sailaway form, with standard kits of parts enabling the owner to add easily to the interior, engine or spinnaker gear as he or she wishes, at any point in the boat's life. A typical modern trailer sailer is shown in fig 5.1.

If you choose a boat that is easy to use as a trailer sailer, you may find that you keep the boat ashore when not in use, especially if you do not use her every weekend. As well as saving on mooring or marina fees, this means that antifouling paint is not really necessary. As the boat is dry-sailed it is much easier to keep the interior dry and in good condition, whilst the exterior should remain free from osmosis. Furthermore, it is easy to move the boat from one sailing area to another, and so you may find yourself exploring more of the coastline than would otherwise be possible. On the other hand, if the boat

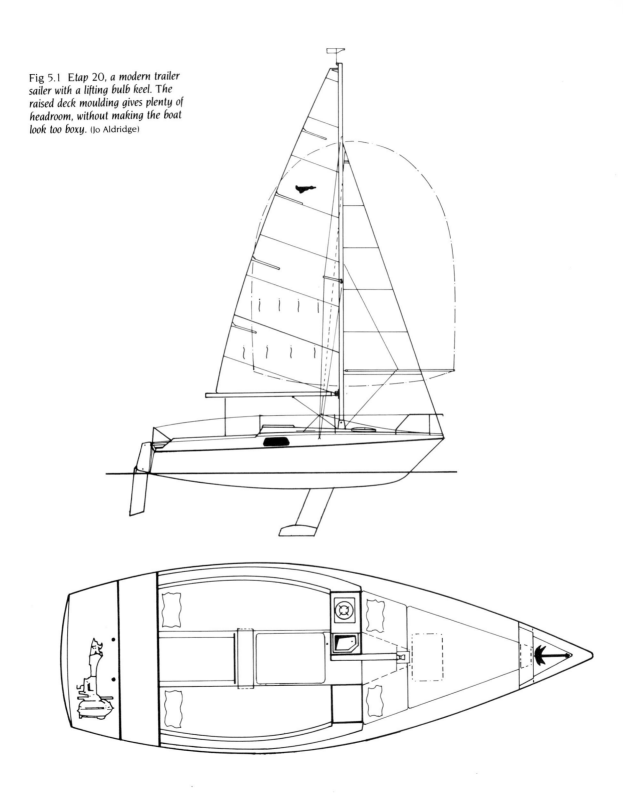

Fig 5.1 Etap 20, a modern trailer sailer with a lifting bulb keel. The raised deck moulding gives plenty of headroom, without making the boat look too boxy. (Jo Aldridge)

should prove difficult to launch and recover, you will probably only put her on the trailer at the end of the season, and keep her in a normal berth or on a mooring for the rest of the time.

Mooring and berthing

Although the boats we are looking at are relatively small and light, they must still be moored or berthed properly. Apart from the risk of breaking free, a badly moored boat will chafe her lines and may also damage herself by rubbing or bumping against the dock.

Let us first of all look at mooring the boat. Most moorings will be laid by the harbour master, yacht club or other local organisation, and so the design and maintenance of the actual mooring tackle need not concern us here. The mooring will either be from a single point at the bows, or at both bow and stern. The latter is becoming much more common, as the boat will not swing around nearly as much and so more boats can be packed into a given stretch of water.

At the bows you will need a fairlead and mooring cleat large enough to take the mooring chain. Cleats where the fastenings pass through feet projecting each side of the cleat are stronger than those where the fastenings go through the body of the cleat, and so are to be preferred. The mooring chain itself needs to be brought on board and fastened round the cleat, as the rope attaching the marker buoy to the chain is seldom strong enough to hold the boat and would soon chafe through. The marker buoy itself can be either left on board or put back in the water.

Either the fairlead should close over the mooring chain, or the chain should be lashed down so that it cannot jump out of the fairlead and saw its way through the gunwale. The rudder also needs to be lashed in place as this will reduce wear on the bearings and also minimise the amount by which the boat swings, especially when the wind blows her across the tide.

When moored at both ends, similar considerations apply, except that there will be a second mooring chain at the stern. You will generally want the fairlead to be on the quarter, so that there is little chance of the chain wrapping itself round the rudder. To avoid rust marks or wear on the deck, it is well worth slitting open a length of large-diameter plastic hose and slipping it over the chain where it lies across the decks.

As rivers and estuaries are becoming more and more crowded, it can become increasingly difficult to find a mooring. Bilge keels or a lifting keel can be a great advantage here. There may be a number of moorings that dry out at low water, and if you can sit on bilge keels, or raise your centreboard and raise your rudder sufficiently, there is no reason why you cannot use one of these berths. The only caveat applies to some bilge-keelers which have the keels moulded in with the hull and the ballast cast in afterwards: if there is no steel shoe on the bottom of the keel, the plastic may quickly wear through. Eventually, the ballast may drop out of the keel and the boat fill up with water. This is particularly likely where scrap steel punchings are used for ballast, simply poured dry into the keel and secured with some resin or plastic over the top.

Mooring to piles is essentially very similar to mooring fore and aft, except that instead of bringing a mooring chain on board you pass your line through a metal ring, that slides up and down a rod on the pile to compensate for the rise and fall of the tide. When tying up, always pass your line through the ring and bring it back on board, so that you do not need to be able to reach the ring when casting off. The trick is to approach one pile, get a line round it, and then carry on to the second pile to get a line round that before stopping and adjusting the lines. If the piles are some distance apart quite a long length of line may be required. Where several boats share a pair of piles each boat will need to be tied onto her neighbour with breast ropes and springs, but unless rough weather is expected only every second or third boat will need to have lines onto the piles.

As the number of marina berths carries on increasing, more and more yachtsmen succumb to the pleasures of being able to tie up alongside the jetty and just step ashore. Here one ties up with a breast rope at each end to keep the bows and stern close in to the berth, and a pair of springs running diagonally to stop the boat moving fore and aft. Ideally, the breast ropes will go from the stem and the quarter for maximum effect, but often the boat is longer than her berth, in which case the after breast rope will need to be moved forwards, so that it still comes square off the mooring cleat onto the jetty. All the lines should be just slack in calm conditions, holding the boat not too tightly against the dock. Nylon rope should be used for the lines as its elasticity means that no sudden shock loads are transferred to the boat. If the same berth is used each time, lines can be made up to length and either kept on board or spliced onto the mooring cleats on the dock.

Ground tackle

The weight of anchor required varies greatly with the wind and sea conditions. What is acceptable when anchoring in a sheltered bay for lunch is totally inadequate in a gale off a lee shore, and to meet these differing requirements most boats will carry both a light and a heavy anchor. It is on the coastal cruising vessel that good anchoring gear is particularly essential, as other boats are less likely to anchor so often. The racing boat will probably head for a mooring or marina berth between races, whilst the ocean sailor will be under way a greater proportion of the time, often in waters too deep to anchor in.

There are four main types of anchor in use, the fisherman's, the Bruce, the plough or CQR, and the Danforth. Whilst the fisherman holds well on very weedy bottoms, where other designs often have problems, its heavy weight and cumbersome shape mean that it is seldom used on small boats. The other three types all have their enthusiastic supporters, and each has its pros and cons. The Bruce is better on a short scope, but its shape makes it difficult to stow. The Danforth is the opposite in this respect, as it stows flat without any problem. However, if it should start to drag it does not bite again very readily, and the CQR is better in this respect.

The anchor may have either an all-chain warp or nylon rope terminated by a short length of chain. The advantages of all-chain anchor warps are that the weight of the chain ensures that the loads on the anchor are horizontal, and the large amount of sag in the line prevents snubbing in rough waters. Chain is also chafe-proof, both at the stem roller and on the bottom. The great disadvantage of chain is its weight, especially as on most boats it is stored right up in the forepeak. Thus, many boats have just a short length of chain to keep the

Table 5.2   Recommended size of ground tackle for boats of different displacement

	Displacement (tons/tonnes)			
	1	2	3	4.5
Anchor (lb)	18 (8 k)	22 (10 k)	26 (12 k)	31 (14 k)
Chain (mm)	6	8	8	8
Rope (mm)	10	14	14	14

pull on the anchor horizontal and to avoid chafe problems. The rope should be three-strand nylon which gives the best combination of strength, high stretch (to absorb shocks) and durability. As a minimum, the chain length needs to be at least that of the boat.

Table 5.2 gives a guide to the size of ground tackle required for the main anchor. The second anchor can be considerably lighter – though no less than half the weight – and equipped with a shorter warp of rope and chain. Ideally, there should be an anchor well in the bows capable of taking one anchor and its warp, so that one can always anchor quickly should the need arise. The well needs to have a strong, well secured lid and large-diameter drainage holes.

When preparing to anchor, one should approach the anchoring point slowly, from either downwind or downtide as appropriate, losing way all the time. When the boat is virtually stationary enough warp can be let out so that the anchor reaches the bottom, and then it should be let out more slowly as the boat begins to drift backwards, until all the required amount of line has been let out. The length of scope needs to be at least three times the depth of water if chain is used or five times for nylon line. In rough weather the scope may need to be doubled on occasion, and in shallow waters more may be needed to prevent the boat's motion being snubbed too violently by the anchor line becoming tight. If it looks as though severe weather is on the way, a second anchor may be laid, either on a second warp or better still with both anchors on the same warp.

The dinghy

Whilst marinas and quay facilities are steadily growing all round the sailing world, there are still many anchorages where the crew need to anchor and make their own way ashore. Although a centreboard or bilge–keel boat can often go right up to the shore and drop the crew off, most boats have a deep enough draft to require a dinghy.

If a dinghy is necessary, there is no room on a small boat for anything other than an inflatable. On short coast-hopping trips it can simply be towed behind the boat without any problems, so long as the drop in performance can be accepted. On longer journeys it can be deflated and stowed in a cockpit locker. When it comes to reinflating it, a small compressor running off the boat's battery makes life much easier.

There is a distinct knack to rowing an inflatable. As it is so light and the hull form has no grip on the water, it stops very quickly. To keep it going one must maintain a rapid succession of short strokes with the oars. On short journeys it often proves easier to sit in the bows and scull, pulling the boat along behind one. But whatever technique is used it is extremely difficult to row into any headwind, and a small outboard motor becomes almost essential. If the yacht also uses an outboard it may prove possible to avoid duplication by using the same one, so long as the revs are kept at a sensible level when it is on the dinghy.

This is perhaps a good point at which to consider the general problem of getting on board the boat when she is not tied alongside, be it from the dinghy, from the water after a swim, or when recovering a man overboard. A rigid ladder extending at least 18 in (46 cm) below the waterline is really essential here. It can be either clamped onto the rail for occasional use, or integrated into the design of the stern so that part of the pushpit is swung down into the water, simultaneously providing a ladder and a gate in the pushpit. Often, the transom is designed with a step at the bottom, providing a small platform for use when loading gear on board or as a swimming platform.

6

OFFSHORE SAILING

Although there is no clear-cut difference between coastal and offshore sailing, the offshore sailor tends to go on longer passages without stopping and sail in more exposed waters as a result. Thus, because of the more exposed waters and the greater distance to a safe haven, the offshore yacht must be of stouter construction, and better equipped and fitted out than a boat that stays close to land and is only sailed at weekends.

Choosing the right boat

Because the majority of yachtsmen are involved in racing or coastal sailing, almost all production boats are designed with these ends in mind – especially small boats, where there is a marked difference in approach between a weekend sailing craft and a boat capable of sailing in exposed waters for weeks on end.

    The first requirement for offshore sailing is good construction, both in the amount of material used and in the standard to which the boat is built. If one is in doubt about the builder's quality control it may be worth engaging a surveyor to supervise construction of the boat. In time, any flexible areas of the deck or hull will succumb to crazing and cracking round hard spots, such as bulkheads or corners in the coachroof. As far as the actual weight of the laminate is concerned, you will have to rely on the designer having done his sums properly, though the availability of a Lloyds Moulding Certificate (or its equivalent if the boat is built abroad) is a good guideline here.

    One worry that many people seem to have is the use of end-grain balsa in a sandwich construction, especially below the waterline. Although the open grain can soak up water if the outer skin is damaged, there will be virtually no migration of water to other areas of the hull, assuming a good quality balsa has been used. The only way in which this could happen is if large areas of the inner or outer skin delaminate from the core, in which case the ensuing loss of structural rigidity will be a much more serious problem.

The actual design parameters of the hull and rig will be fairly conservative. Although it is exciting to sail a lightweight boat for a day or two, after a while the very responsiveness and quick motion of the boat becomes fatiguing. Furthermore, a light boat's performance will be affected to a far greater extent by the weight of stores necessary for extended voyages than that of a heavier displacement boat. Although people have sailed boats that are basically dinghies on long cruises, it requires a great deal of stamina and motivation, more than most people are likely to possess. For long-term cruising, many people would consider even a 30-ft boat on the small side for a crew of two, due to the lack of living space, the increased likelihood of capsizing in extreme conditions, the slower passage times and the quicker motion of the boat. Against this, many small boats like the Vertue (fig. 6.1) have made extensive voyages, and for many people there is more satisfaction to be had in completing a passage in a small boat than in a larger one, as well as appreciable financial advantages. Perhaps the biggest deciding factor is the length of time one will spend continuously on board. If the intention is to live on board, a considerably larger boat is needed than one which will only be inhabited for three or four weeks at a stretch.

Thus, the boat will be of moderately heavy displacement, but with enough canvas to make her a good performer in all conditions. The hull will be of moderate proportions, with bow sections that are full enough and have enough freeboard to lift to the waves and keep the foredeck dry, and with the stern balanced against the bows so that the boat remains well behaved at all angles of heel. The midship section will not be flared excessively, as this would make the boat more sensitive to heel and so the crew would have to spend an excessive amount of time changing sails to keep the boat within the optimum range of heel angles. If this is taken too far, though, one ends up with a very slim boat that has little volume down

Fig 6.1 *Vertue mk II, a classic long-keel cruiser, in production from the 1930s to the 1960s, and sailed across the Atlantic and most other oceans.* (Jo Aldridge)

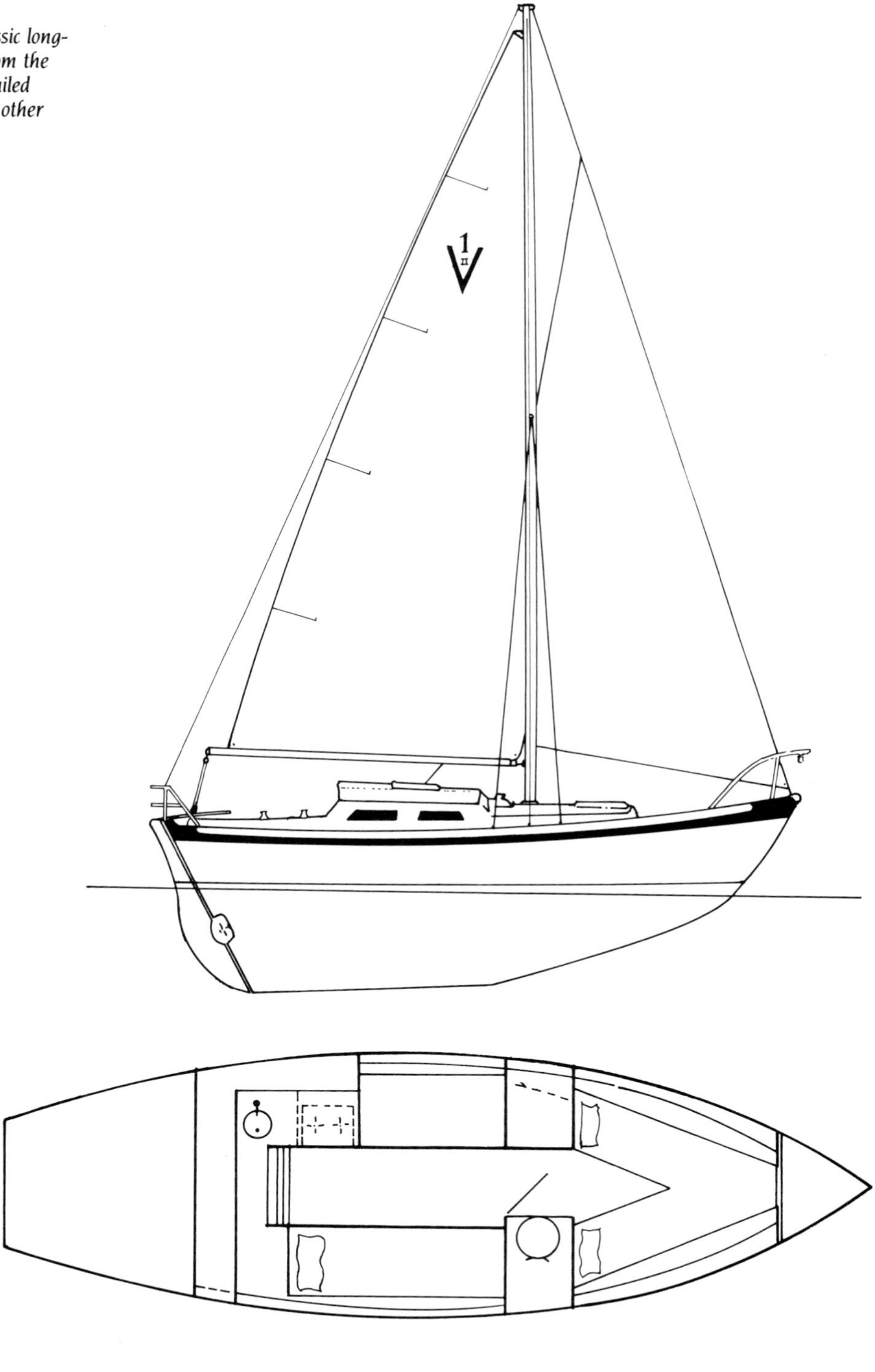

below for the accommodation, and it will also sail at large angles of heel, which will quickly tire the crew out.

As far as the deck is concerned, there will probably be a deep sheltered cockpit to keep the crew relatively dry and safe. Good cockpit drains are essential, but, although an open transom offers the ultimate solution, the increased exposure of the crew and the increased likelihood of having gear swept out of the stern mean that this is far from ideal. The deck will also have adequate handholds and harness clip-on points, especially around the mast and foredeck where the crew will work, together with jacklines running from the cockpit to the stem. It should be possible to clip onto a secure point before leaving the cabin, and then to clip on to the jackline from the security of the cockpit (twin harness lines are a great help here). The jacklines should be placed as far inboard as possible, as the aim is to keep the crew on board rather than keep them attached to the boat when they fall over the side.

Timing the passage

One of the most crucial factors on a long cruise is to be able to estimate the journey time accurately. As a guide, cruisers have speed:length ratios somewhere between 0.75 and 1.0, giving a run of 80 to 105 miles in 24 hours for a boat with a 20-ft (6-m) waterline. The variation will depend partly on the design of the boat, and partly on the wind speed and direction. This is only a guide, though. If becalmed, the crew can keep the boat's speed up by motoring, and if a fast passage is made there is, of course, all the more time to explore the pleasures ashore.

Deck layout and sail handling

The deck layout of an offshore yacht has to be planned with concern for the security of the crew uppermost, together with ease of working when short-handed. As we have seen, this means a relatively deep and snug cockpit, with deep coamings. Furthermore, the coachroof should not be too wide, so that there is plenty of space on the side decks.

Whilst it is preferable to lead all the lines aft to the cockpit when the boat is fully crewed, this is not the best solution when short-handed. In this case, it pays to keep the halyards and reefing gear on the mast. With this arrangement, one person can change headsails, or take in or shake out a reef in the mainsail, without too many problems. With the conventional layout where everything is led aft, to do these tasks would require at least two people – one in the cockpit to handle the halyards and reef lines, and another forward to gather the sail or take in the reef.

The mainsail must be capable of three reefs, with the third one good and deep, so that the next stage would be to take down the entire mainsail. It should not have much roach, and the battens can be longer than those permitted by racing rules, as a large unsupported roach rapidly reduces the life of the sail. A robust topping lift should also be fitted, both to support the boom in harbour, and to double as a spare mainsail halyard.

All the sails should be made out of a soft fabric, without a heavily resinated finish. These will be much easier to handle, have a longer life span, and stow in a much more compact space than the highly resinated sails used by racing sailors, let alone the Mylar and Kevlar fabrics used at the front of the fleet.

Reefing

With the likelihood of stronger winds and larger waves offshore, a little more care needs to be taken over the rig than usual. Much of this comes down to common sense, and to spending that little bit of extra time on every operation to make sure that it is done properly, but there are some tips worth knowing.

As far as reefing gear for the mainsail is concerned, slab reefing is to be preferred for shortening sail, due its maintaining an efficient sail shape at all times. To prevent the boom hitting the deck when reefing, one of the rigid kicking straps that support the boom is worth considering. The drawback with using a topping lift is that in the long term it will chafe the leech of the mainsail. On the luff of the sail, slides make it easier to hoist or lower, but much of this advantage is lost if the sail has to be taken out of the luff track to set the trysail, or if some slides need to be taken out of the track when taking in a deep reef. Once the sail is set, the bolt rope is less prone to failure, as it is attached to the sail over the entire length of the luff and so no highly stressed eyelets can pull out. Because of this, my preference is for a luff grove rope on a boat of this size where the sail is not so large as to be difficult to handle.

With headsails, the choice lies between conventional headsail changing and a roller-reefing sail, and if conventional sails are used one has the choice between hanks or a headfoil. Roller reefing is always a great temptation for short-handed sailing, as the crew escape the need to go on the foredeck in rough weather. All that is required to reef the sail is to ease the jib sheet (though not by so much that the sail flogs) and wind in the reefing line, preferably on a self-tailing winch. To set more sail, the opposite procedure is followed: the reef line is eased and if necessary the sail is helped to unfurl by winching in the jib sheet. If the sail is cut correctly, with a relatively high clew, there should be no need to move the position of the genoa sheet car.

The price to pay for this ease of handling is that, as the sail is reefed, it also becomes fuller – the opposite to what is required. Also, because they are continuously exposed to the wind and sun, the foot and leech of the sail deteriorate very rapidly. Perhaps the most serious situation, though, is if the gear jams when the wind is increasing. If the sail is partly furled it may prove impossible to furl it completely, or to unfurl it and drop it. However, the loads on the gear on the size of boat we are dealing with are relatively small, and so the risk of failure is much less than on a larger boat.

Perhaps the best procedure with roller-reefing gear is to have a large overlapping genoa for light and moderate winds, which is then changed to a smaller working jib as the wind increases, and the latter is then roller-reefed when it is necessary to reduce sail further. On larger boats, especially those requiring a fairly large sail plan due to their heavy displacement, a cutter rig may be worth considering with roller furling gear on both foresails.

However, as the headsails on smaller yachts are not very large, particularly with a fractional rig, I do not think roller reefing is the right answer. Instead, I would use a number of hanked-on genoas: a light-medium number-one, 135 per cent number-two, 105 per cent number-three and a storm jib on a fractional rigged boat; a number-one, number-three, heavy-weather jib and storm jib on a masthead-rigged boat. The use of hanks means that there is no possibility of a sail falling overboard while being changed, and that it is possible to have a second headsail clipped onto the forestay ready for a sail change if necessary. I would not use a twin forestay, as it is very difficult to keep a tight jib luff with this arrangement, and when changing sail the hanks of one sail often catch on those of the other.

When sailing to windward with a mainsail reefed so that the head comes some distance below the hounds, leech tension tends to put a reverse bend in the mast, and the backstay is generally too high up to help much. If you have a babystay, which is unlikely on a boat of this size, simply tensioning it so that the mast has some forwards bend will avoid the problem, though you may need to pull the babystay tight on a winch if it only has a three- or four-to-one rope tackle. Failing this, you will have to use the spinnaker pole topping lift, making it fast on the stem fitting or some other strong point well forward and winching it in until the mast is bending the right way.

With a fractional rig, though, it is debatable how effective a deep reef is, at least for sailing to windward. This is because the top of the sail is cut with much more round in the luff, as the mast bends that much more above the hounds when the full main is set. Once reefed, the luff round just makes the sail excessively full because the mast is straighter lower down. Thus, for a long windward leg it may well be worth going straight from the second reef in the main to the trysail, especially if the wind is going to continue rising.

Self-steering gear

On a small boat some form of self-steering gear is almost essential on long passages. It enables sails to be changed or navigation to be carried out without calling extra hands up on deck, thereby greatly helping the crew sail for extended periods without becoming excessively tired. Having said this, though, the crew cannot leave it all up to the autopilot: a proper watch must be maintained at all times.

Vane steering gear is relatively large and cumbersome for a small boat, and the large number of mechanical linkages makes the equipment relatively expensive. Thus, most owners are happy to put their trust in an electric self-steering system, despite the need for a steady power supply. In the size of boat we are concerned with, these systems generally consist of an actuator arm dropping into locating sockets on the tiller and the the cockpit side, with an electronic compass for course setting (fig. 6.2). The more sophisticated units also have the ability to steer to a wind vane, which is virtually essential when sailing close-hauled.

The point to watch on all these units is the waterproofing, as water has a tendency to seep through the sealing rings on the actuator arm or the controls, whereupon it wreaks havoc with the electronics. To help avoid these problems, the control unit

Fig 6.2 *This compact autopilot simply drops into brackets on the tiller and side of the cockpit.* (Photo Nautech Ltd)

can often be mounted inside the cabin and the actuator should not be left on deck when not in use.

Watch systems

The key to enjoying any extended passage is often the watch system: well planned and well executed, and everyone arrives in port fresh and ready to taste the delights of shore; a poor system, and as soon as the boat is tied up everyone falls asleep.

For day sailing or an overnight passage there is no great need for a formal rigid watch system. If the crew know each other, and each other's capabilities, then when one crew member has had enough he or she can be relieved by the most rested crew member. This system can work well so long as all the crew are prepared to pull their weight. It also helps if the more experienced members are divided evenly between watches, so that one or two are on deck at all times.

A similar approach is often used on racing boats. With the majority of races lasting 72 hours or less, a very flexible approach can be used, so long as the crew are fresh at the start of the race and have time to catch up on their sleep after the finish. The aim is primarily to have enough people on deck at any one time to carry out all the sail trimming, and have the resources to call up enough people to do a sail change – generally the whole crew on a small boat. The off watch crew can sleep down below in light airs or off the wind, using whichever bunks give the correct fore-and-aft trim. On the wind or close reaching in a breeze, though, when stability is required, they will generally doze on the rail, clipped on by their safety harnesses so that they cannot fall overboard when asleep or in those few moments of disorientation when waking.

The actual watch system can work in one of two ways: either there can be a strict rotation, with crew coming on watch at set times, or crew members can be paired off in a 'buddy' system, so that when a crew member needs a break he wakes his buddy. In the first case, a new crew member will generally come on watch every one and a half or two hours, as the new man helps keeps the crew driving the boat and the disruption of a change of watch is minimised. The crew rota will also be decided so that people with similar skills and levels of experience are on different watches. The buddy system relies on a responsible approach by all the crew if they are not to collapse half-way through the race, but it does offer greater flexibility. Once again, the crew should be paired off as helmsmen, sail-trimmers and navigators.

On a cruising boat the crew generally want to have some energy left at the end of the passage, and so such a hard driving approach is totally out of place. A formal watch system is required, with the off watch crew having the freedom to stay on deck or have a sleep down below. Generally the crew is split up into two, three or four watches. In a two-watch system there will be equal periods of three or four hours alternately on and off watch; if there are three watches each man will have two hours on and four hours off; in the case of four watches they will have two hours on and six off. The actual number of watches will depend on the number of crew on board and the number needed on watch at any one time, determined by the length of the passage and the sailing conditions. The more watches, the more rest the crew get, but the fewer crew on deck. There is no reason why the same watch system needs to be maintained throughout a passage, however, and the wise skipper will vary the watch system to suit the conditions and the state of the crew. Also, one of those on watch can be on standby, so that for the first or last part of his watch he can stay below and rest, oilskins at the ready so that he can come back on deck if required.

The watches may either change all at once, or one member at a time. Whilst the former system is the traditional one, the latter helps to keep the crew on deck fresh and alert, and also minimises the disruption down below. Four people getting in and out of oilskins at the same time in a 26-footer (8 m) is quite a crowd.

Two functions have a special place in any watch system, the cook and the navigator. The easiest system is to have two of each, standing opposite watches so that at any one time there is a cook and navigator on watch. Alternatively, one crew member can be both cook and navigator, not standing any fixed watch, but cooking and navigating as required and being on standby whenever an extra pair of hands is needed.

The engine

For extended cruising an inboard engine is more or less essential these days, not so much for the extra propulsive power it offers over an outboard, but because it is the most convenient means of recharging the batteries. In this respect, it is often worth fitting a more powerful alternator to the engine than the standard size.

Other forms of recharging the batteries are also viable, such as solar panels, windmills or water powered units. These are generally all preferable to using the engine, but they do have limitations and so they can only be regarded as a means of augmenting the engine's capacity, rather than replacing it. Perhaps the ideal arrangement is a combination of solar panels and a windmill, as what the more temperate regions lack in sunshine they generally make up for in wind.

One important factor in any engine installation is the capacity of the fuel tank. As a rough guide, a small diesel engine will consume about 0.06 gall. (0.27 l) per horsepower for every hour that it runs, and a petrol engine will need double this quantity. Thus, if we assume that on average an engine is run for a couple of hours a day at half power to recharge the batteries and for general motoring, a 10-horsepower engine will consume 4 or 5 gall. (18–23 l) of diesel in a week. Thus, a fuel tank capacity of at least 20 gall. (90 l) will be required for serious cruising, or about 40 gall. (180 l) if a petrol outboard engine is used. This is best divided into two independent tanks or kept partly in separate jerrycans, so that if a tank should leak or water should get into the fuel the engine can still be used. Each tank should have a drain tap underneath it, so that if the fuel does become contaminated it can easily be drained off.

Stowage

One of the major problems in a small boat is that of finding enough stowage space. Thus, when preparing for a voyage one must first decide if there is room to carry all the gear, and if necessary prune the list of items to a more acceptable length. Then a stowage plan must be drawn up, so that the more frequently needed items are most accessible. The stowage also affects the boat's motion in a seaway: if the weight is distributed throughout the length of the boat, her motion will be more sedate and comfortable. If the weight is too spread out, though, the boat's performance will suffer, and the slower motion will mean that she may not rise to the waves in a short sea. A boat with longer overhangs and fuller ends, particularly at the bows, will suffer less in this respect than a fine-ended boat, which needs all the help that she can get to lift to a wave.

The other danger when stowing a large amount of gear is to the boat's fore and aft trim. As the forepeak is perhaps the least habitable part of the boat in a seaway, the temptation is simply to store as much gear as possible up forward, thus depressing the bows. Upwind, this will probably make the steering steadier, but the boat's performance may suffer slightly. Off the wind, the bows will lose much of their dynamic lift and so, instead of lifting as the boat accelerates, they may dig in and start a broach.

Storm survival tactics

As we have already seen in Chapter 2, small boats are much more prone to being knocked down or capsizing in storms than

Fig 6.3 A model yacht in a test tank, simulating the boat's behaviour in breaking waves, in research sponsored by the RORC. With no sea anchor the boat lies beam onto the sea, and is rolled over onto her beam ends and capsized.
(Photo RoRC)

larger craft, because the waves are the same size no matter how small the boat. Thus, heavy weather is a particular problem for small craft from the naval architect's viewpoint. Furthermore, the more violent motion and the cramped living quarters of a small boat increase crew fatigue, and so the stamina of the ship's company is another important factor.

As far as boat handling is concerned, there are two basic approaches: run before the storm or heave-to with a sea anchor or streaming warps. Both aim at achieving the same effect, namely keeping the boat sufficiently bow- or stern-on to the waves to avoid going broadside-on, either by broaching or by being blown broadside on by the wind.

Whilst the correct approach must to some extent depend upon the boat's design, it appears that both tactics have their uses. When the waves are steep, due to a confused sea, a newly developed storm or shallow water, then the boat is in most danger of broaching, due to the conflict in water flow between the crest and the trough of a wave. The best option here is to stream warps or a sea anchor, which will keep the boat sailing slowly and will also stop the stern swinging round. However, when the waves are longer – for example, in deep water or when the storm has been blowing for a while – the wavelength will be much greater, and so the water flow will be more or less the same throughout the length of the boat. Therefore, here the best option is generally to run before the storm as fast as can safely be done, as this minimises the speed of the waves relative to the boat. Whichever method is used, one must always aim at keeping the boat at the correct angle to the waves.

A few more words on the sea anchor. At one time it was deemed to be an essential item for weathering out a storm, but these days it has largely fallen into disuse. As just discussed, it can usefully be deployed to slow the boat down and thus keep her in the correct attitude to the waves. It also appears that it can be of great assistance in preventing the boat capsizing in breaking waves, if streamed from the weather quarter when running or broad reaching to the waves. If the boat should start to be rolled the sea anchor will immediately provide both a strong righting moment and a pull on the stern helping the boat lie stern on to the wave, as the rolling of the boat tries to

Fig 6.4 *The same boat with a sea anchor deployed from the stern. This helps to swing her stern onto the breaking sea, reducing the likelihood of her being capsized even if the cockpit is swamped.*
(Photo RoRC)

pull the sea anchor through the water. This can often be sufficient to keep the boat on her feet. To be at all effective, it does need to be large and let out on a long line from the boat so that it is always well submerged, with a swivel to let it spin without twisting the line.

7

RACING

Yacht racing can be at many different levels – from a club's end of season fun race right through to an IOR level rating world championships – and the owner interested in racing must first of all decide at what level he wishes to campaign. This will determine the type of boat he will sail, his budget, his crew and the amount of time he will spend involved with the boat, both on and off the water.

One-design racing

This is perhaps the best form of racing for most sailors, except for the fact that the choice of boat is limited to the one-design classes sailed in your area.

One-design classes are based on the supposition that all boats racing will be essentially the same. However this is seldom absolutely true as most classes allow a choice of sailmaker, some variation in deck layout, and perhaps a number of different options regarding the interior. Thus, if entering a one design class it is a good idea to look around at the winning boats and see what modifications have been made to the boat from the standard specification.

There are quite a number of classes with local one-design racing, but relatively few have strong class racing nationally or internationally. This is because most successful one-designs are not competitive under rules like the IOR as by definition they cannot be developed, whereas even production boats can have alterations made to displacement and rig dimensions relatively easily to keep up to date. Thus, unless strong fleets are established within the first year or two, the class will only spread slowly to new areas, as new owners will be at a disadvantage racing under the IOR while a fleet is being built up.

The type of boat that develops into a one-design class varies greatly, from fast overgrown dinghies, such as the J-24, that are best suited to sailing in sheltered waters, to comfortable, seaworthy little cruisers, such as the Sonata (fig 7.1). The point is that, as all the boats are virtually identical, there is no need to have a high-performance design to give good racing. In fact, some people would say that if you are having to spend a lot of the time concentrating on boat speed you are losing out on the tactical side, which is one of the strong points of one-design racing.

Apart from the advantages of not being bound by the vagaries of any handicap rule and often the cost benefits of being in a one-design class, it is the closeness of the racing that is the main attraction in one-design sailing. One is sailing boat-for-boat with the rest of the fleet, which results in plenty of good close tactical sailing, rather than against the clock.

Channel Handicap

Channel Handicap was originally devised by the RORC and UNCL as a simple handicap system that would introduce owners to racing at no great cost, and entice them to enter the realms of the IOR. However, it was clear from the start that most owners who raced under the scheme were not interested in selling their family cruiser and investing a much larger sum of money in a boat that was competitive under the IOR, in order to race in a class where they might well be outclassed by sailors whose sole interest in sailing was in winning races. Thus, Channel Handicap has attracted a fleet that is now considerably larger than the British IOR fleet, offering cheap racing at club level under a rule that rates reasonably accurately a much wider range of designs than the IOR caters for. Many owners of outdated IOR designs are realizing this and changing down to Channel Handicap.

The rule has two interesting features: first of all, the owner measures up his own boat; secondly, the actual rating formulae used are kept secret. Although some may think that having the owner supply his own boat's measurements lays the rule open to abuse, by cross-checking against manufacturer's specifications, IOR measurements and Channel Handicap certificates of

Fig 7.1 Sonata 7, a popular one-
design class that combines
performance with close racing and
good handling characteristics.
(Jo Aldridge)

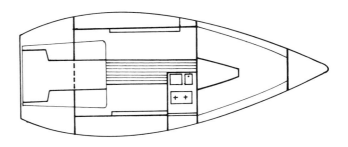

sister ships, virtually all dubious measurements are detected and corrected before the certificate is issued. The formulae are a closely guarded secret so as to try and avoid designers coming up with boats that are designed to cheat the rule, and they are updated every year to improve their accuracy. Thus, whilst it is not possible to analyse the rule as closely as the IOR, it is clear that the rule favours the more moderate type of cruiser–racer in preference to ultra-lightweight designs.

The Channel Handicap System is also very strong on the safety side. Each boat has a basic safety number calculated for it, based on length, beam, displacement and sail area, which tries to assess the fundamental seaworthiness of the design (see fig 7.2). The owner can then improve upon this by carrying safety equipment to various levels, having a self-draining cockpit and other similar features. The race committee can then specify a minimum number for boats entering a race, depending upon the waters it will be sailed in. This is surely a much more realistic approach than just imposing a minimum length or rating for the event.

International Offshore Rule

The IOR at one stage catered for all levels of yacht racing relatively successfully. But over the past few years it has become increasingly apparent that standard production boats with amateur crews are seldom as competitive as one-off boats with quasi-professional crews of people who have enough time to practise until they are near perfect, often thanks to the owner paying generous expenses. This is not to say that one approach to racing is better than the other, but just to point out the current trend and the approach that is required to win.

In relation to the rest of the sailing fleet IOR boats are relatively light and over-canvassed, with a narrow waterline beam and highly flared sections to give a fast boat with plenty of stability from the crew weight. They are demanding boats to sail well, but they can be very exciting and rewarding as a result. Although some critics claim that they are not as seaworthy as more moderate designs, to a large extent this depends upon how well they are sailed. They definitely cannot be hove to and left to look after themselves *in extremis*, but they

Fig 7.2 *Channel Handicap System certificate. The SSS numeral is an index of seaworthiness, the TCF is the time correcting factor. The section near the bottom of the certificate is for rig penalties.*

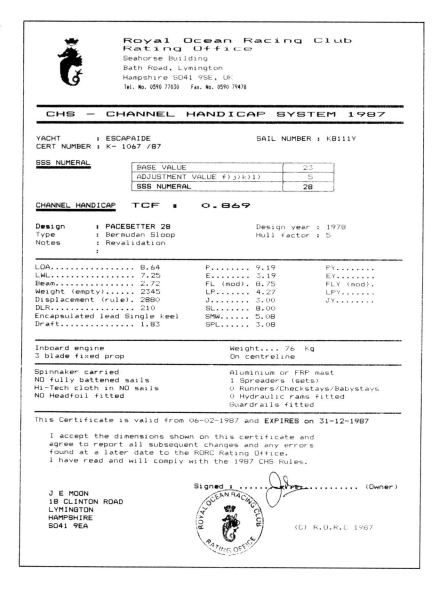

must be sailed and steered carefully through even the worst weather. As a result, in the hands of the inexperienced they are definitely not exceptionally seaworthy, but in the hands of an energetic and experienced crew there should be few problems. In bad weather most of the incidents that occur are the result of sailmakers, spar-makers or designers trying to save

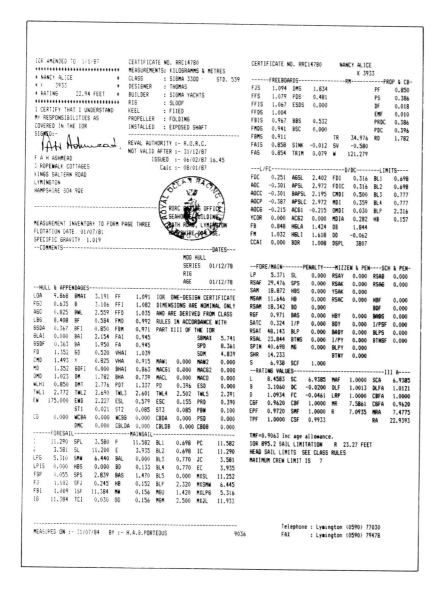

Fig 7.3 IOR *certificate. The rating in feet is near the top left-hand corner, and the time multiplication factor (TMF) is near the bottom right. As the boat in this case belongs to a one-design class, the measurements are standardised.*

too much weight and consequently compromising the boat's structural integrity.

IOR racing has clearly split into two camps now. First of all, there is the traditional offshore racing involving races of at least 100 miles, either across the Channel or along the coast. Here, the main components for success are a good navigator, a fast boat and a crew that has enough stamina to keep driving the boat all through the race, even if it lasts several days. On the other hand, there are the 'round-the-cans' races, where boat for boat tactics, mark rounding and boat handling are at a premium. As the boats in the IOR fleet become lighter, more sensitive to crew weight and more stripped-out down below, true offshore racing is becoming less popular at the top of the fleet. However, less serious races that finish at an interesting foreign port, such as those laid on by the Junior Offshore Group (JOG), are remaining popular. Perhaps in the end we will see the top end of the IOR fleet restrict itself to short inshore races, whilst Channel Handicap takes over offshore racing.

International Measurement System

IMS is a rule that was developed in the USA by a group of yachtsmen who were disillusioned with the contorted shapes and narrow type-forming generated by the IOR. The main feature of this rule is its high mathematical content, though one wonders whether yacht design has been sufficiently quantified for this approach to be fully justified. Thus, the hull is measured by a special device that measures several hundred points on the boat and feeds their offsets into a computer, which fairs them out to produce a lines plan. This is then analysed to give the hull and rig form parameters, and through a whole volume of formulae the rule tries to predict the boat's performance over a range of wind conditions. Then, this data is reduced to a number of different handicap figures, and the race organisers can elect to use either one overall mean figure or the figure which corresponds to the type of course and the mean wind strength.

Although I can see the appeal of this high-tech approach, there are two drawbacks. Firstly, comparing the boat's predicted performance against that actually achieved often shows errors of one knot or more. Secondly, it will cost at least as much to measure a boat from scratch under this system as it will to measure a boat under the IOR. Admittedly once a number of boats to one design have been measured, their hull figures will be applied to all sister ships, and boat builders may be persuaded to bear the cost of the initial measurements. However, if one looks at any cruiser–racer fleet, it immediately becomes obvious that most of the boats racing are no longer in production. I cannot see their owners being prepared to spend a large sum of money to get measured while they still have the alternative of Channel Handicap or some local handicapping rule.

Design philosophy

The approach to designing an out-and-out racing boat is very different from that to designing a cruising boat. The first stage is to analyse the rule by comparing the performance attainable from a variety of combinations of length, beam, sail area, displacement and stability against the rating. The aim of this is not necessarily to come up with a fast boat, but one that will have better speed than that predicted by the rating formulae.

Once the basic dimensions of the boat have been selected, the next stage is to develop the lines plan and rig, once again trying to get the most out of the rule. The deck layout comes next, and here the designer has two aims: to ensure that the crew will be able to adjust the rig easily, preferably from the windward side; and to create a large cockpit that will give the crew enough space to work without getting in each other's way during tacks, gybes and sail changes. It is only at this stage that the interior layout is considered, and nowadays this is generally kept to the minimum that is functional and complies with the requirements of the rule.

As far as construction is concerned, this is kept as light as possible so that the weight can be centralised, to reduce resistance when sailing in waves. This explains why racing boats often have large amounts of internal ballast, which they cannot put into the keel without being penalised for being too stable.

Horses for courses

Every boat has strengths and weaknesses in its performance. The very nature of yacht design means that each boat must be a compromise between light- and strong-wind performance, beating and offwind efficiency. Coupled to the different emphasis that the various rating formulae place on design parameters such as length, beam, displacement and sail area, this makes designing a good, competitive boat to a rating rule quite a complex business. However, it is clear that a design must be suited to one particular measurement rule, as the bumps on an IOR boat will not affect the IMS rating, whereas the fullness of the ends of the boat, used by both the IOR and the IMS, will not affect a Channel Handicap certificate, for example.

Once a rating formula has been in existence for a while, designers quickly get to grips with its strengths and weaknesses, and can start designing boats to exploit the rule. On the one hand, this consists in distorting the hull and rig parameters to suit the rule's measurement methods; on the other hand, the boat can be designed to have particular strengths in her performance. Thus, when asked to design a boat for a particular event or even to sail in a particular area, the designer will collect data on wind strengths and wave heights, and also on the types of courses to be sailed. From this, the boat will be designed to be better on particular points of sail or wind strengths than the majority of the fleet. This must be done with some care, though, as he dare not let the performance in other areas suffer too much, in case the weather does not behave as expected. An example of the effect of departing from the norm can be seen by looking back at earlier IOR designs. Being relatively heavy and fine-ended, with a masthead rig, if kept up to date over the years they generally out-perform modern designs upwind in a blow and running in light winds. However, in most other conditions the more modern designs are much faster. So, whilst the older boats can win a race given the right conditions, for the most part they are no longer really competitive.

Another factor often underestimated by owners and designers alike is the effect that the wind strength has on the handicapping system. In light winds the difference in speed between large and small boats will be much less than in strong winds, as the smaller boats will reach their maximum boat speed at a lower windspeed than large boats. Thus, if sailing in an area with predominantly light winds it will pay to have a boat at the smaller end of the rating band for one's class, whilst in areas with stronger winds it pays to be at the upper end. Perhaps the ideal solution, if entering individual races rather than a series, is to be right on the borderline between two classes, and 'tweak' the rating in accordance with the weather forecast between races – for example, by moving a measurement band between races, so that one always has the best rating!

Deck layout

The deck layout on racing yachts is becoming increasingly standardised. There is a simple trench throughout the length of the cockpit, interrupted only by the mainsheet traveller. At the sides of the cockpit there are footrests for the helmsman and mainsheet trimmer to brace themselves against. The rest of the crew sit out on the rail unless actually required in the cockpit to adjust something. The cockpit is generally large and shallow to give the crew plenty of room to work in and to make it as easy as possible to move across the boat, which inevitably results in the coachroof being well forwards.

Because of the importance in keeping the crew to weather in a small boat, all rig controls will be led to both sides of the boat, so that they can be operated without the crew having to come in off the rail. As well as keeping the weight in the right place, this also generally results in quicker alterations to the rig settings. Genoa sheet cars will be free-running on the tracks, with control lines led to the cockpit. The genoa sheets will often be led across the boat to a winch on the windward side, so that all the crew weight is to weather as the boat comes out of a tack, and also so that the sail can be adjusted quickly and easily once the crew have settled down.

At the mast, the genoa and spinnaker halyards will emerge some 7 ft (2.1 m) above deck level, enabling the crew to heave down on them rapidly at the mast. Then they will be led aft to the cockpit, except that in the smaller boats the spinnaker halyard may just be cleated on the mast, if one man can hoist the sail from there. On some boats the spinnaker halyards may be crossed over inside the mast. The lead at the top is better if the leeward one is used, but it is easier to hoist the sail if the crew is working from the windward side, so crossing the halyards over makes a lot of sense once the crew have become used to it.

The genoa tracks may run fore-and-aft or athwartships. A barber hauler, for fore-and-aft adjustment, mounted on an athwartships track appears at first to give more control over the sail's sheeting angle, but with use a number of disadvantages become apparent. First of all, the long distance between the clew of the sail and a fixed sheeting point (the barber hauler is not fixed) means that the sheeting angle tends to vary a bit between the gusts and lulls. Second, it is seldom possible to bring the sail in as far inboard, as the barber hauler sags off to leeward when the sail is drawing. Thirdly, the tracks are more critical in their positioning, and heavier due to their extra length, than longitudinal tracks.

In my opinion, the best solution is to have short longitudinal tracks for each sail, with a barber hauler in the form of a small snatch block as a lazy block on the genoa sheet, led out to the rail. This is a much more stable sheeting arrangement and, although there is not so much control over the sheeting when the sail is trimmed to the rail, the sheeting is less critical when sailing off the wind.

Crew numbers

For a number of reasons, racing boats tend to carry more crew than their cruising cousins. Although it results in a heavier boat, therefore with more resistance to motion, this is offset by a number of mitigating factors.

First of all, most racing occurs round relatively short courses, with frequent mark roundings and sail changes. Here the sheer manpower of a larger crew results in faster manoeuvres, so long as the boat is well laid out and the cockpit is large enough for all the crew to work in. Secondly, racing boats tend to be relatively unstable, either because of rating rules such as the IOR, or because boats like the J-24 have been designed with high sail area:displacement ratios to make them exciting to sail. In all but the lightest winds, the additional stability gained by carrying extra crew members out on the weather rail allows the rig to be powered up more, and the extra driving force from the sails more than offsets the increase in hull resistance.

Fig 7.4 *Deck layout of a quarter-tonner. The genoa fairleads can be easily adjusted from the cockpit. Because of the small size of the genoa, winches are only needed for snubbing and trimming, so the bottom action winches permit small adjustments to be made easily without the need to spend time putting in the winch handle.* (Photo Tony Castro)

The extent to which a large crew improves boat performance is shown by the presence of crew limitation factors in the IOR and most one-design fleets. Without it, much larger crews would quickly become the norm. For example, a Tartan Ten, which is a very narrow and lightweight 30-footer (9 m), may well race in Channel Handicap with nine crew members in windy conditions, in order to have the stability she needs when beating and reaching.

The crew should not be a fixed mass who park themselves on the weather rail and stay there till the next tack. They should move inboard in every lull and out again in the gusts, to keep the boat on her feet. Also, moving the crew forwards will lift the stern and improve performance in light airs, whilst bringing them aft will give the boat stability and help keep the rudder immersed in a blow. Upwind, most boats perform best with the crew relatively far forward to keep the forefoot immersed. The exception to this is some of the lighter flat-bottomed IOR boats, which go faster with the crew aft, though the bows will tend to wander a bit as they are struck by waves. This is particularly the case if the boat has been given a large amount of bow-down trim for rating reasons.

The racing rig

One of the biggest differences between the crew of a cruising and that of a racing boat is that whilst the former are happy to set their sails and adjust them only periodically, the racing crew will be adjusting their rig continuously to get the best performance out of the boat at all times. Therefore, they have evolved a rig that is very responsive, but in its more extreme forms must be handled carefully to avoid gear failure.

Whilst all small racing keelboats are fractional-rigged these days, two distinct types of rig have developed, due to a mixture of influences of the formulae of the IOR and developments in the dinghy and dayboat fleets. First of all, there is the IOR rig, where the spreaders come square off the mast and the rig is supported fore-and-aft by the forestay and runners, with the backstay and checkstays being used simply to control mast bend. Secondly there is the rig that has developed in one-designs such as the J-24, where the spreaders are swept back and the rig is supported by a combination of the forestay, shrouds and backstay. Although this rig is less controllable than the IOR rig, the absence of runners makes it much easier to handle for less experienced crews.

Fractional rig with runners

Dealing first of all with the IOR type of rig, as the spreaders and shrouds are not swept aft they have virtually no effect on the fore and aft bend of the mast, and so they can be set up independently. The upper shrouds should be set up with enough tension so that the mast does not sag off to leeward in a breeze, and accordingly the upper shroud tension should be increased until the leeward upper shroud is only just slack when on the wind. The lowers and intermediates should then be adjusted so that the mast below the hounds is straight in light to moderate winds, with the top only bending off slightly at higher wind speeds. This can easily be checked by sighting up the mast when sailing on the wind. If you find it impossible to keep the mast straight, you may well find that the problem lies in the spreaders being too short, or, in a double spreader rig, in them being out of proportion to each other.

If jumpers or diamonds are fitted, the amount of tension required is dependent upon the stiffness of the top of the mast. The more tapered a mast is above the hounds, the more support it will need, and so the tighter the jumper wires. If too slack, the top of the mast will whip about too much whenever the boat hits a wave, and in a gust the bending of the mast will open up the leech and spill all the power from the sail. On the other hand, if the jumpers are too tight then the rig will be too rigid, and on hitting a gust the mast will not give at all, resulting in the boat heeling excessively instead of staying on her feet and accelerating away. Furthermore, it will not be possible to flatten off the head of the mainsail in strong winds.

The mast will be keel-stepped and rigidly held at deck level. By controlling the forestay length, the heel position and the mast partners, the amount of pre-bend and rake in the mast can be adjusted to suit the mainsail and the balance of the boat. Then, when sailing, the runners have the dual effect of controlling the shape of the genoa through the forestay sag, and of increasing the amount of mast bend due to the extra compression loads induced by tightening the runners. The checkstays are then used to limit the mast bend, whilst the backstay de-powers the main by flattening off the head of the sail and opening up the leech. If you find that you only need the checkstays to stop the mast pumping in a seaway, you probably have too little pre-bend in the mast and should increase it by lengthening the forestay, chocking the mast forwards at deck level or moving the heel aft.

When sailing at the lower end of a headsail's wind range, or off the wind with the genoa up, easing the runners will increase the forestay sag and thus increase the fullness of the sail. Then, when running under spinnaker, the mast can be raked forwards by clipping a spare halyard to the stem and winding it in, which helps to prevent stalling of the air flow around the sails.

The other major rig control, particularly with Kevlar mainsails, is the amount of mainsheet tension. On a racing boat, as the sheet tension is transmitted up the leech of the sail to the masthead, it increases mast bend and pulls the fullness out of the sail, and so flattens off the sail without opening the leech up. Thus, as the wind increases one needs to increase the sheet tension steadily, and play the traveller to de-power the rig in the gusts. However, on a boat with a more cruising-orientated rig, increasing the mainsheet tension will merely tighten the leech, and not flatten the sail off to any great extent.

Fractional rig with aft-swept spreaders

If the rig has swept spreaders instead of runners, there is not such a clear division into fore-and-aft and athwartships control. Thus, because the backstay tension controls both the forestay sag and the amount of mastbend, it is much more difficult to set the rig up to perform well in all conditions. The only way round this, where permitted by class rules, is to rig up a purchase on the forestay and lead it back to the cockpit.

To obtain the best performance from the rig, it usually pays to alter the standing rigging to suit the prevailing conditions, just as one would on a dinghy. In light airs, some sag is needed in the forestay to power-up the headsail. However, to stop the mainsail back-winding the mast often needs some bend in it, to flatten the entry of the sail. Thus little backstay is used, and the mast is bent by chocking it forwards at deck level, easing off the lowers, and perhaps raking the spreaders further aft. As the wind increases, though, a straighter forestay is required, and the problem becomes one of maximising the forestay tension while preventing the mast bending too much. The mast also needs to be held rigidly, so that it does not pump due to the waves. Now the opposite techniques are applied: chock the mast back, tighten the cap shrouds and lowers (and jumpers if fitted), and swing the spreaders forwards so that they are in line with, or perhaps slightly forwards of, the shrouds.

At the same time as paying attention to the balance between mast bend and forestay sag, the athwartships behaviour of the mast must be controlled. Although the variations in rig tension may make this appear a difficult task, as the boats are generally single spreader rig the masts are relatively stiff athwartships, and so a reasonable compromise can be found. The main control here is the length of the spreaders, but if starting from scratch with a new mast then moving them up and down will control the position from which the top of the mast sags off to leeward, and therefore how much the leech opens in stronger winds. Raising the spreaders effectively stiffens the top of the rig, though if taken too far the loads on the gooseneck may cause control problems lower down the spar.

Racing sails

The cut and design of racing sails are very different from those of their cruising counterparts. This is because, whilst the cruising yachtsman prefers sails which will have a long working life at minimal outlay, and which are made from a softer, more easily handled sailcloth, the racing yachtsman is only interested in one thing – speed.

As a result, racing sails are made from very hard, stable materials: either a very closely woven, highly resinated nylon or polyester; or, for still better performance at higher cost, a cloth of polyester or Kevlar, either bonded to one side or sandwiched between two layers of Mylar. Generally, the more exotic the cloth, the stronger and more stable it will be, giving a lighter sail with a more precisely controlled shape. But this is often achieved at the expense of a shorter life expectancy and a greater chance of it disintegrating quickly, instead of just becoming increasingly tired.

The other difference between cruising and racing sails is the wide variety of cuts of racing sails. Although there is without doubt an element of fashion behind some of the cuts, there is a more serious purpose behind them. Firstly, the use of radial panels helps spread the loads from the corner of the sail into the body of it, without distorting the light cloth. Similarly, the highly loaded leech is generally made from a double-ply, or a strongly uni-directional cloth aligned with the direction of loading, whilst the luff and the lower part of the mainsail can be made out of a much lighter cloth . Secondly, the aim is to control the shape of the sail, so that the fibre orientation helps the sail become progressively flatter as the wind increases.

Mainsail

In a fractional rig, the mainsail is without doubt the key sail. It is also the hardest sail to cut satisfactorily, as one sail has to cover the entire wind range. This is to some extent offset by the wide control the crew have over the sail through the clew outhaul and flattener, the Cunningham hole, the mainsheet and traveller, the backstay, runners and checkstays. Unfortunately much of this control is lost as the sail is reefed, for a number of reasons. To start with, the top of the mast bends more than the middle, and so reefing results in a fuller head to the sail. Secondly, the backstay has less effect on the sail, and so it cannot be used to flatten off the head and free the leech. Thus, it pays to keep the full main up for as long as possible, flattening it out by bending the mast and increasing the sheet tension, and controlling it by playing the traveller.

Generally it pays to keep the full mainsail at least until the number-three genoa is set, and in flat water it often pays to hold it whilst headsails are changed down to the storm jib. This is because whilst large headsails provide a large driving force, they also provide a large heeling force. However if the headsail is too small in relation to the mainsail, the airflow is not steadied over the sails sufficiently when the boat pitches, and so efficiency drops off.

Fig 7.5 Sailing on MG 26 upwind at full power. All the crew are sitting the boat out except the helmsman. The sails are just beginning to be twisted off to depower the rig – the genoa could have a little more twist to match the mainsail.

Headsails

In inshore races the key headsails are the number-one and number three. The number-two is of more use offshore, as its sheeting angle is limited by the spreader length, and in flat water the better pointing ability of the number-three more than makes up for its smaller area. All genoas down to the number-three should be full-length on the luff, with the overlap going from the standard 150 per cent of the number-one, down to 135 per cent for the number-two, and 105 per cent for the number-three, so that it fills the foretriangle completely. Beyond this point, the luff will be reduced slowly, but the sails will retain the high aspect ratio of the number-three for good windward performance.

Spinnakers
Although most spinnakers are still made of nylon, sails based on Mylar and other plastic films are becoming increasingly common. These materials are particularly advantageous for light weather spinnakers, as water from rain or spray just runs off the sail, instead of soaking into the sailcloth and weighing down the sail to stop it filling properly. These fabrics are also less elastic, so the cloth does not distort when a gust hits it, and their lack of porosity means that air cannot seep through to the low-pressure side. Unfortunately, these sails tend to collapse easily with the shock loadings that occur when the boat hits a wave, but the effect can be minimised by putting a length of shockcord onto the head of the sail, and attaching the halyard to this.

Spinnakers were the first sails to utilise radial construction, at first in the head and then in the clews. Most sails still have horizontal panels in the middle to control the shape of the sail, but this is slowly giving way to tri-radial sails, or sails with vertical panels in the middle of the sail aligned with the leech. These result in a stronger, more stable sail which flattens out with increasing sheet tension. However, the extra complexities involved in determining the panel shapes has limited the development of many sail cut patterns, these only becoming feasible with the development of computer-aided design techniques.

Weight distribution

A boat sailing through waves can be represented as a see-saw, pivoted in the middle and with weights at each end. Next time you are playing with your children in the park, put them on the ends of the see-saw and set it in motion. Now move the children in towards the middle, and you will find it considerably easier to start and stop the see-saw. In the same way, if a boat has all her weight close to her centre of gravity, about which she moves in waves, a lot less energy is needed to make her climb each one. As the sails only supply a finite amount of energy, the boat with all her weight amidships will have better performance than one with the weight spread throughout her length.

In the case of IOR and IMS designs, which have their stability measured, reducing the weight of the rig and decks also helps lower the centre of gravity, and so the boat can have a lighter, slimmer keel with more of her weight carried in the form of internal ballast.

The major influences on the weight distribution are the rig, followed by the keel. Thus, if sailing in exposed waters it is worth going for a light, relatively large-diameter mast, with the minimum weight of rigging and instruments at the masthead. Similarly, it is worth going for a keel that has most of its mass high up, possibly with a wooden lower half, so long as the boat still has sufficient stability.

Next, there is the hull. The distribution of much of its weight is determined during construction, and the use of lightweight materials like Kevlar/epoxy/foam sandwich or light softwoods like Western Red Cedar in racing boats is a direct result of attempts to centralise the weight of the boat by building as light a hull as possible, and then bringing the boat up to weight by means of internal ballast.

For the same reason, the weight of the accommodation is kept to a minimum, and wherever possible it is fitted out with foam or honeycomb cored boards to give a structurally strong but very lightweight interior. Fittings, running rigging and so on also need to be kept light, but strength should not be sacrificed, as time lost by gear failure (if the race can be finished at all) will almost always be more than the time saved by better weight distribution.

Finally, there are the crew themselves. They should keep as close together in the boat as possible. This is particularly the case in lighter boats, as the crew make up a larger proportion of the all-up weight. Look at any well sailed two-man dinghy, and you will see that the helmsman and crew sit as close together as possible.

Sail handling and manoeuvres

The key to successful crewing on a racing boat is teamwork, and nothing can beat practising regularly with the same crew. This way, everyone knows what they and everyone else will be doing during a given operation, and no time is wasted talking the crew through it beforehand.

Tacking

The simplest operation is tacking. Here, when the helmsman or tactician decides to tack, the crew should remain on the rail until the last moment to keep the boat upright and driving. Then, as the tack starts, they come in, and one crew member eases off the old genoa sheet as the luff starts to break, while another pulls in the new one as the boat goes about. Assuming he is reasonably fit, the entire sail can be pulled round and sheeted in without using the winch, which is only necessary if he is slow in pulling the sail round so that it fills with wind too soon, or for final trimming of the sail. If at all possible, the genoa sheet should be sheeted to the weather side, so that as much as possible of the crew weight is up to weather as the boat comes out of the tack. At this point the boat is travelling relatively slowly, and in a blow will tend to heel excessively and stop in a blow.

While this is going on, the mainsheet should be pulled in to the centreline as the boat comes into the tack, thus helping the boat to head up into the wind, and then eased out a little beyond its normal setting on the new tack, until the boat is at her normal angle of heel and is picking up speed. When tacking, the runner man has an easy job, as the wind is putting all the load onto the forestay. However, he must not ease the old runner before the boat has come up into the wind, and, whilst the new runner needs to be brought in tight quickly, keeping it at a little less than full tension will give the sails that little extra drive as the boat comes out of the tack.

The actual speed with which the helmsman tacks the boat depends primarily on the crew – they must be able to work fast enough to keep up with the boat – but also on the design. Tacking too slowly means that the boat speed will drop off too much during the tack, whereas spinning her round too quickly will stall out the keel and rudder, and so the boat will sag off to leeward out of the tack until the water flow has reattached itself. Once round, it will pay to sail slightly free at first to build up boat speed, so that the keel is not overloaded by the combination of a high side force from the sails and not enough boat speed to create lift.

De-powering the rig

Before resorting to sail changes, there is a lot that can be done to de-power the rig before a change is necessary. The headsail can be flattened by applying a lot of runner tension. (A load cell on the forestay with a read-out in the cockpit helps ensure consistency between tacks, but the final say must be had by the sail-trimmer, as he is the only one who can see the genoa properly.) Increasing runner tension will also tend to increase mast bend, and so, whilst easing the checkstays will flatten the mainsail, enough checkstay must be kept on for the sail to retain some flow, and to prevent it inverting. Applying tension to the backstay will also flatten the head of the sail and open up the mainsail leech, whilst the flattener will flatten the lower third of the sail. All of these alterations, together with the higher wind speed, will move the fullness aft in the sail, and so the Cunningham hole should be tightened up to keep the draft in the correct place.

Returning to the headsail, allowing the clew to rise by easing off the barber hauler or moving the sheet lead aft will de-power the sail by letting the leech twist off, and sheeting it outboard will also de-power it, at the expense of pointing (though VMG will probably be better in a rough sea). Increasing sheet tension will also lesson the draft of the sail. Ideally, the twist and set of the mainsail and genoa should be matched to each other, because twisting off the main with a tight-leeched genoa will just increase backwinding, whilst the opposite will mean that there is no slot effect near the head of the genoa.

All of these operations can be done by one crew member coming inboard, with all the others staying to weather to keep the boat upright.

If you find that the main traveller needs to be eased so much in gusts that the backwinding of the mainsail extends right aft to the leech, it is definitely time to change down. (If your mainsail is still relatively full, and you have done as much as possible to flatten it off, then the mast probably needs a little more pre-bend, or less tension in the lowers, to help it bend more.) On a short windward leg, though, it often pays to try and hang on, rather than accept the loss in boatspeed that is inevitable when reefing or changing headsails. This is why it is so important to ensure that you have the correct headsail set at the beginning of the leg on short races.

Reefing

To take a reef in, one crew member is needed by the mast, and one on the main halyard and kicking strap. The main halyard is eased, and the mast man pulls the sail down either to put the reef cringle onto a tack hook, or to attach a second Cunningham tackle to the reef cringle. The kicking strap and mainsheet are eased, and the man on the halyard now winds in the reef line until it is tight. Finally, the lines are made fast, the mainsheet and kicking strap pulled in again, and the leech line adjusted. The mast man's work is made much easier if he can pull the sail down on the weather side, so the reefing gear really needs to be accessible from both sides of the sail.

Shaking a reef out is really just the reverse process. The reef line is let out, and the halyard eased just enough for the mast man to pull it off the tack hook (or the Cunningham is eased if that method is used). The sail is then hoisted up, with the kicking strap and mainsheet eased for the last few inches.

Headsail changes

The easiest form of headsail change is the tack change, though the ease of sail handling must be balanced against the strategic consequences of a tack, and the possibility of being caught on port tack by another boat when in mid-change. First of all, the boat must be on whichever tack puts the spare halyard and headfoil groove to weather. The new sail is brought up to the weather rail in its bag, and if properly flaked the corners of the sail should be close to the bag openings. A sheet is now passed through the new sail's fairlead and attached, using either a spare sheet or the weather sheet of the existing sail, while the bowman unclips the halyard from the mast. He now takes the sail forward, feeds the head into the luff groove and attaches the halyard (with the cockpit man taking the slack out of the halyard to prevent it snagging round a spreader end). Now the sail can come out of its bag and be hoisted, so that it lies against the weather side of the old headsail – during the hoist, the bowman attaches the tack of the sail to the stem fitting. As soon as the sail is up, the boat tacks, and the old sail is dropped to the deck. It can now be flaked into its bag, either on the weather rail or down below. Generally, it is better to take the sail off the foredeck to flake it than to have the bowman spend time on the foredeck securing the sail.

If a tack change is not possible, either the new sail will be hoisted to leeward of the existing one, or the old sail will be dropped to leeward of the new one. Both of these operations are considerably more difficult than a tack change, and so on a long offshore leg the arguments for putting in a short hitch when doing a headsail change are quite strong. In particular, when dropping a sail to leeward of the new one, you may well find that a second person is required up forward, one to pull the sail down at the luff, and the other to pull it in and under the other sail at about mid-length. Apart from this, the procedures are really exactly the same as with a tack change, except that when setting the new sail to leeward the halyard must be taken round the leech and outboard of the existing sail, to prevent the two halyards becoming twisted.

Reaching

As the boat comes off the wind, the main traveller comes to the limit of its travel, and so the kicking strap needs to be used to adjust the twist in the sail, with the mainsheet adjusting the boom's angle to the centreline. Also, the genoa will need to be sheeted further outboard, either by means of a barber hauler or by putting a snatch block on the rail – if this is not done the sail will have too much twist, and also the leech of a number-one genoa will hook up to weather too much. If a snatch block is to be used, or the fairlead has to be adjusted, one should try to think ahead and make the changes on the opposite tack, so that the crewman's weight remains to weather. In windy conditions the trim of the sails can have more effect over which way the boat goes than the rudder, and for the best boat speed it is definitely better to minimise the helm movements, so the crew should be adjusting the mainsheet, genoa sheet and kicking strap continuously, as required by the helmsman.

Spinnaker gear

As the boat comes further off the wind, a spinnaker will be set. Most of the horror stories told about spinnakers involve hoisting, gybing or dropping the sail, and the key to a successful operation is always good preparation.   The actual layout of spinnaker gear can vary quite considerably between boats. On a small boat, though, the sail is small enough for successful dinghy systems to be copied. Thus the pole will be end-for-ended during the gybes, with the downhaul led to the base of the mast so that it does not need adjusting each time the guy is trimmed. Alternatively, on a racing boat the downhaul can be dispensed with, and the guy led well forwards, so that it doubles as the downhaul. Although simpler, with this arrangement the pole will tend to drop when a gust hits the sail, and also if the guy is eased too far too quickly the pole can lift uncontrollably.

The pole can be stowed in a number of ways. It can be clipped to the base of the mast, with the forward end lying free on the foredeck. On cruising boats that use the spinnaker less

Fig 7.6 *This quarter-tonner has a fly-away spinnaker pole system that stows itself along the main boom, just like in a racing dinghy. Only one pair of sheets are used, with tweakers for pulling the weather sheet down.* (Photo Tony Castro)

frequently it will be stowed along one side of the foredeck. Lastly, on out-and-out racing boats it can be stowed alongside the main boom, taking weight off the bows, and avoiding the need to adjust the pole lift and downhaul or to go onto the foredeck to clip on the guy, each time the sail is to be set.

This last approach can be taken one step further, with a fly-away pole system. Instead of being reversible, the pole will have a rope attached to the inboard end, that will pass through a fitting on the mast and back to the cockpit. Pulling on this line will set up the pole by pulling it forwards, along the boom and onto the mast fitting. To stow the pole, the line is released and the pole knocked off the mast fitting, whereupon shockcord pulls it back along the boom. Although this system is probably less efficient when gybing, it does make it much quicker to set the pole when short-handed.

Setting the spinnaker

Let us start off with the simplest case of hoisting the sail on a run without having to gybe. Before arriving at the mark where one will bear away and set the sail, one should clip the spinnaker bag in place, and attach the halyard, sheet and guy. If beating up to the mark, with a bit of forethought this can be done on the tack opposite to the one on which the spinnaker will be set, so that the crew weight is kept to weather. The pole can also be set once the navigator is certain that no further tacks or gybes will be required. Then, as the boat comes into the mark, the sail is hoisted and the guy pulled round. The sheet should not be pulled right in before the sail is hoisted fully, to prevent the sail filling before the sail is hoisted. During all this, the mainsail needs to be let off quickly to help the boat bear off, and the genoa should also be eased. Finally, once the sail is up and drawing, the genoa will be dropped onto the foredeck and secured with some shockcord, unless it is only a small headsail, which can often be left up with no detrimental effect on the spinnaker.

As can be seen, a large number of pairs of hands are required to make the operation run smoothly. Either the runner man will take the mainsheet, or the helmsman may take it and the runner man move forward into the cockpit. There will generally be one person on the halyard, one on the guy and one on the genoa and spinnaker sheets. If there is anyone left, the bowman can pull on the halyard at the mast.

Hoisting on a reach is basically the same as hoisting on a run, except that in a breeze it is all too easy to over-trim the sail as it is hoisted, whereupon the boat may broach or be pinned down by the sail. In these conditions it will pay to bear off slightly at the point when the sail is partly hoisted until it is all set properly and under control. The other danger is the guy: it must be eased enough so that the pole is just off the forestay, but the crew must allow for the rope to stretch as it comes under load.

If beating up to the mark it is generally best to avoid having to tack around it just before setting the spinnaker, but this is sometimes inevitable. In this case, the inboard end of the pole can be clipped onto the mast before the mark, the boat tacked, and then the outboard end raised as the boat rounds.

Finally, it may be necessary to gybe when setting the spinnaker. Here, the boat must bear off onto a run and gybe before the pole can be set properly. However, once again the inboard end of the pole can be clipped on in preparation, and one can often start hoisting the spinnaker before the genoa is gybed. Unfortunately, in this situation less hands are available, as the runner man is fully occupied during the gybe, and in a breeze the helmsman may not be able to gybe the main at the same time as steering the boat.

Gybing

The spinnaker gybe is largely controlled by the foredeck hand. In preparation for the gybe, one man must be on the runners and one on the mainsheet (unless the helmsman is handling this). In addition, if twin sheets and guys are used then one person needs to be on the sheets and one on the guys. If 'tweakers' are used instead, then one man will be on the sheets, and the tweakers can be pulled tight on both sides before the gybe, and the leeward one let off after it. The bowman will be standing by the mast, with the genoa sheet and lazy guy to hand.

Once the boat is on a dead run, the foredeck hand releases the old guy from the pole, and unclips the pole from the mast. From now on, the man on the spinnaker sheets must watch the sail all the time, playing the sheets to try and keep the sail filled until the gybe is completed. As the pole comes inboard, the genoa sheet from the side on which the pole will be set is slipped over the end of the pole, while the other genoa sheet slides off. The sheet or lazy guy is now clipped into the pole end, and the pole is pushed out and forwards onto the mast. During this process, the cockpit crew must ensure that the pole downhaul is eased a foot (30 cm) or so, and the new guy or sheet is not so tight as to prevent the pole being pushed out. The helmsman must also keep the boat on a run until the pole is on the mast. Meanwhile, back in the cockpit, the boom will have been swung across, and the lazy guy or the leeward 'tweaker' let off.

If the leg is a long one, or if it is known that a number of gybes will be required, the foredeck hand can forget about the jib sheets. These can be sorted out on the last gybe, or if necessary undone from the sail and thrown over the pole so that they lie over the outboard end of the pole when the end of the leg is reached.

Although it is the spinnaker that creates the major complications when gybing, the mainsail and runners also require attention. The mainsail should be pulled part of the way in, flicked across the boat as soon as the wind has got the wrong side of it, and let right out immediately on the new gybe. Trying to send it across too early, or not letting the sail right out immediately, may result in the boat broaching up to weather.

The runners may either be led forwards under the boom when running, or up over the boom and across the leech of the sail. The latter arrangement is safer in heavy weather, as more runner can be pulled in before the gybe, but the runners will chafe the mainsail, and pull the leach up in light airs. Taking the runner under the boom means that it needs to be pulled in more quickly on the gybe, and the boom must be absolutely free of any obstructions that the runners could catch on, but the sail will set better and the leech of the mainsail cannot be damaged. Perhaps the best way of handling the runners is to have one turn round the winch of each runner, and stand in the middle of the boat with one rope tail in each hand. Then, as one sees the boom swing inboard, one can pull in the new runner, so that it is hand tight by the time the boom reaches the centreline. Once the new runner is taught, the old one can be released from the winch, and in anything of a breeze it will be pulled out by the momentum of the mainsail. If in doubt, taking the slack out of the backstay gives a slightly greater margin of safety when gybing in heavy weather.

Lowering the spinnaker

When it comes to lowering the spinnaker, the rate at which the halyard is eased is crucial. If we once again begin with the simple case, dropping the sail and hardening up, the first job is to set up the mainsail controls such as clew outhaul and Cunningham. Then pull the genoa round to the leeward side of the foredeck, check the genoa sheets, and hoist the sail. Next, coming in to the mark, one person goes to leeward to pull the spinnaker in, holding the sheet or lazy guy until he can reach the sail; one mans the halyard, ensuring it has a couple of turns round the winch and also that the tail is free to run; and a third person is on the guy. The guy can either be allowed to run forward, still attached to the sail, or it can be tripped from the sail at the pole end. Letting it run is quicker in the first instance, and keeps weight off the foredeck, but then the guy does generally need to be re-rove after the sail is dropped. Tripping requires the pole to be eased far enough forwards for the bowman to reach the pole end, which is a disadvantage on the run.

When all is ready, the guy is let off so that the sail blows out to leeward, and the halyard is eased. At first, quite a lot of halyard must be let off, so that the sail collapses and the crew can bring it in to the boat, but then lowering must be slowed down so that the sail is not allowed to fall into the water. The pole can be left alone for the moment, though the runner, mainsheet and genoa sheet will all need to be hardened in as the boat is brought onto the wind. Once the spinnaker drop has started, each crew member should move up to weather as soon as he has completed his task, as the boat's angle of heel will rapidly increase as she heads up. In the end, there should only be one crewman off the rail, to lower the pole, tidy up the ropes, and repack the sail.

If the boat has to tack as soon as she has hardened up, the same basic procedure applies. However, before the drop the bowman must ensure that the weather jib sheet lies over the pole. And when dropping the sail it helps if it can be pulled in under rather than over the jib sheets, as in this way it does not interfere with the sheets when the boat tacks. Also, in addition to dropping the sail, the crew must lower the outboard end of the spinnaker pole as soon as the guy is slack, so that the helmsman is free to tack at any time.

Where the boat is coming in to gybe immediately before the mark, there are two options: either one can play safe, and drop the sail in comfort just before the gybe; or one can do a 'float drop', whereby the spinnaker pole is removed and stowed before the gybe, the boat is gybed, and then the spinnaker is pulled down as the boat rounds the mark. If in doubt, it is best to play safe and drop the sail before the gybe. However, a float drop, if properly executed, keeps the sail pulling right up to the mark, and the drop is made simpler by the absence of the pole. Against this, it is dependent on the skill of the sheet trimmers to keep the sail full all the time – without a pole the chances of getting it to set again after collapsing are relatively slim.

Spinnaker changes

Finally, we come to changing spinnakers. There are two basic approaches here: to drop one sail and then hoist the new one; or to 'peel', hoisting the new one before dropping the old one.

Lowering the old sail first is the simpler procedure, especially on a run. The new sail is got ready on the leeward side of the foredeck, with the halyard and a spare sheet attached. Then the old sail is dropped onto the foredeck, where it is gathered by one crew member, while another unclips the guy and clips it onto the new sail. As soon as the guy is on, the new sail can be hoisted, and the guy squared back again. This procedure is very quick on a small boat, and there is little chance of anything going seriously wrong.

When doing a spinnaker peel, the new spinnaker is again clipped on forward, with a spare sheet and halyard. To avoid crossing the halyards, the new sail will be hoisted to leeward of the old one if the windward halyard is already in use. If the leeward halyard is the one already being used the new halyard will have to be taken round the forestay in order to hoist the sail inside the old one, if a twist is to be avoided.

The next stage is for the 'peeling strop' to be rigged. This is a line 3 or 4 ft (0.9–1.2 m) long with snap shackles on each end. One end is attached to the tack of the new spinnaker, and then the strop is hitched to or wrapped round the pulpit or headfoil and the other end attached to the stem.

Now all is ready, and the new sail is hoisted and trimmed. Next, the pole is eased forward, the guy is released and the old sail is dropped and gathered. While this is going on, the bowman takes the guy (still passing through the pole end) and clips it onto the tack of the sail, and then trips the peeling strop. If all has gone well you have the second spinnaker flying, with no tangles. However, it is evident that more co-ordination and forethought is required than when dropping the old sail before hoisting the new, and the amount of crew work is considerably greater. Thus, dropping and rehoisting is the better option when sailing short-handed or with an inexperienced crew. It also pays in very light winds, as all the commotion of setting the new sail when peeling generally results in the old one collapsing in these conditions.

8

WINDING UP

As we have seen, there is a wide range in the type of sailing that can be done in a small yacht, from skimming round the estuary in an overgrown dinghy, to packing one's kit bag and going on a world cruise, with many other possibilities in between. Each of these types of sailing has its own attractions, and they need not be mutually exclusive. In fact, each type of sailor probably has a great deal to learn from the others, and should not be too dismissive of those who take a different approach to the sport. Racing yachtsmen have built up a large amount of knowledge on sail setting and handling, coastal sailors on inshore navigation, and the long-distance sailor knows a lot about living on board for extended periods. Each of these skills is only a part of the total required for good seamanship, even though each branch of the sport lays greater emphasis on one set of skills or another.

The most important requirement when selecting a boat is to be honest with oneself, and to see beyond through the image projected by the boat and its attendant salesman so that one can assess if it will really suit one's needs.

The problem is that two designs may have similar proportions and appearance, but one may turn out to be a pleasure to sail, whereas sailing the other may not be at all satisfying – and even the most hard-bitten racing crews are still meant to sail for pleasure. The difference between designs lies all too often in the details, and not the broad concept. Having the winches well-positioned, or ample room in the berths, makes much more difference to the success of a boat than an extra 1 per cent in the sail area: displacement ratio. This obviously holds true on a cruising boat, but even on a racing boat the crew's performance has a far greater effect on the boat's results than the finer points of the rating.

To begin with, the best way of building up experience is to crew on as many different boats as possible, doing as many different types of sailing as possible. There is little point in starting off buying a boat straight away, and then finding that it is not suited to your purposes. Even if you do not intend to race, spending a few weekends on a racing boat may well teach you a lot about nuances of sail trimming and handling. Conversely, if the racing man goes cruising he may discover that seamanship has a wider meaning than just getting round the course as quickly as possible without sustaining gear damage.

When it comes to buying a boat of their own, most people will choose between a second-hand boat and a new production boat. If well maintained, a second-hand boat built of modern materials need not deteriorate with age, and can be in almost as good condition as when new. Thus there is no necessity to go for a new boat, unless it is for the prestige of a spanking new boat in the marina, or because of the appearance of a design that is an improvement on those already on the market. New designs have, in particular, made great developments over the past few years in the use of the interior space. On the other hand, many new production designs these days try to be all things to all men, and end up meeting few requirements completely satisfactorily.

The other possibility is for a one-off boat. After a number of years sailing, one may feel that there is no production boat that can completely meet one's needs, and be tempted into getting a one-off. Although a one-off is more expensive than a production boat, the cost difference can often be no more than 15 or 20 per cent of the cost of an equivalent production boat. The crucial factor if taking this route is the choice of designer: finding one who will have the time and willingness to listen to your needs and ideas, and so produce the boat you want rather than the one he wants. He will also be in a good position to recommend a builder, as he will probably have dealt with a large number of yards over the years, and he should be prepared to check on the progress of the boat as she is built. All too often details that look fine on the drawing board do not work out in practice, and it is generally better to have the designer resolve the situation than leave it to the boat builder.

Fig 8.1 *Dehler 31 – The high coamings and raised cockpit give plenty of room in the quarter berth.* (Photo Dehler Yachts)

The most important thing to remember with a one-off is that in order to keep the costs down the boat must be kept simple. The cost of the hull and rig are relatively constant on all boats, but a complex deck structure, or a large amount of detailed joinery inside the boat, can easily make costs rocket.

When money is tight, one may be tempted to build the boat oneself, either from scratch or from a moulded hull and deck. You may also want to make it yourself for the sheer pleasure of doing so. The amount saved can be as much as 50 per cent on a completed boat, but this must be weighed against the time involved – perhaps a couple of months of full-time work to finish off a bare hull – and the question of the standard of finish must also be considered, both from the viewpoint of the structural safety of the boat, and the effect it may have on the boat's resale value.

Many cruising yachtsmen decry the effect of the IOR on modern yacht design. Whilst racing boats are great fun to sail, and safe in the right hands, the modern one-off design can hardly be described as a good cruising boat. Unfortunately, the blame is slightly misplaced: it lies with the owners, crew and designers who have, naturally enough, explored every possible avenue to gain an advantage under the rule in a climate of intense competitiveness. Some believe that the introduction of a new rule, such as the IMS, will resolve the problem; I believe that the only way it can be resolved is by reducing the level of competitiveness, which would be counter-productive. Thus, the answer would be to let the Grand Prix racer and the cruiser follow their own paths.

In the long term, more and more designs will become available in mass-produced form, which will bring down the cost of buying a boat, and result in a more polished, better designed product. However, this will inevitably also result in some loss of individuality in the designs, as they will have to have more mass appeal than some of the more individualistic designs presently produced in relatively small numbers.

In time, one will probably want to move up to something a little larger than the boats we have been discussing in this book, especially if your interests lie in cruising or offshore racing. This will immediately give considerably more space down below, and a slower, easier motion in open waters. Furthermore the extra turn of speed will enable you to extend your cruising grounds considerably. Against this, the costs rise more quickly than the size of the boat, and the extra size of the sails makes sailing harder work, even though bigger winches are fitted. Furthermore, much of the immediacy and responsiveness that is so appealing in a small boat will be lost, and the deeper draft of a larger boat may prevent you from finding your way into many of the smaller anchorages.

INDEX